STANDING OUR GROUND

STANDING OUR GROUND

A MOTHER'S STORY

Lucy McBath

with Rosemarie Robotham

SIMON & SCHUSTER

NEW YORK   LONDON   TORONTO   SYDNEY   NEW DELHI

37 INK

SIMON &
SCHUSTER

An Imprint of Simon & Schuster, Inc.
1230 Avenue of the Americas
New York, NY 10020

First 37 INK/Simon & Schuster trade paperback edition November 2020

37 INK/SIMON & SCHUSTER and colophon are trademarks of Simon & Schuster, Inc.

For information about special discounts for bulk purchases, please contact Simon & Schuster Special Sales at 1-866-506-1949 or business@simonandschuster.com.

The Simon & Schuster Speakers Bureau can bring authors to your live event. For more information, or to book an event, contact the Simon & Schuster Speakers Bureau at 1-866-248-3049 or visit our website at www.simonspeakers.com.

Interior design by Michelle Marchese

Manufactured in the United States of America

10 9 8 7 6 5 4 3 2 1

Library of Congress Cataloging-in-Publication Data is available.

ISBN 978-1-5011-8778-0
ISBN 978-1-5011-8779-7 (pbk)
ISBN 978-1-5011-8780-3 (ebook)

To Jordan, whose eye is on the sparrow
and I know he watches me.
To Curtis, who walks in faith beside me.
To my family, who never lets me fall.

->><-

"Tell the priests who carry the ark of the covenant:
'When you reach the edge of the Jordan's waters,
go and stand in the river.'"

—Joshua 3:8 NIV

CONTENTS

Preface to the Paperback Edition   *ix*

Introduction: In Guns We Trust   *1*

PART ONE: THE PROMISE

CHAPTER 1:   Black Friday   *11*

CHAPTER 2:   Civil Rights Baby   *27*

CHAPTER 3:   Stones from the River *44*

CHAPTER 4:   Caregiver   *54*

CHAPTER 5:   Paper Boat   *61*

CHAPTER 6:   Finding Faith   *68*

CHAPTER 7:   Love Again   *77*

PART TWO: LOUD MUSIC

CHAPTER 8:   Fast Traps   *93*

CHAPTER 9:   A Hard Choice   *107*

CHAPTER 10:   Premonition   *117*

CHAPTER 11:   Ten Bullets   *128*

CHAPTER 12:   The Right to Exist   *139*

CHAPTER 13:   A Wider Lens   *148*

CHAPTER 14:   Every Mom   *157*

CONTENTS

PART THREE: AWAKENING

CHAPTER 15: A Long-Held Secret   *165*

CHAPTER 16: The Color of Justice   *172*

CHAPTER 17: A Jury of His Peers   *183*

CHAPTER 18: God, the Protector   *194*

CHAPTER 19: Hope Dealers   *204*

CHAPTER 20: Say Their Names   *213*

Epilogue: The Letter   *225*

Appendix: Get Involved   *229*

Acknowledgments   *231*

Notes   *235*

Marching Orders

AT THE TIME I WROTE this book, I had not yet contemplated running for public office. I was a mother who had lost her teenage son to gun violence. Activated by overwhelming pain to *do something*, I became a national spokesperson for gun safety. I could not allow my Jordan to have died in vain. But the mass shootings kept happening. Women kept dying by guns in the hands of abusers. Suicides by firearm remained devastatingly high. And then came Parkland, Florida: seventeen dead at Marjory Stoneman Douglas High School on Valentine's Day 2018, the deadliest high school shooting in our nation's history. In the aftermath, I dared to believe that this time—surely *this* time—public officials would ban assault rifles and require proper vetting of gun buyers to ensure responsible stewardship of such lethal firepower. But, as had occurred so many times before, politicians sent "thoughts and prayers" to the grieving families and failed to follow through.

In 2016, Hillary Clinton had managed to move the needle forward. The first presidential candidate ever to make gun safety a robust part of her platform, she brought together mothers whose children had died by gun violence. We were the Mothers of the Movement, campaign surrogates on a mission to raise awareness of the fact that gun violence affects us all. Two years later, the Parkland survivors aligned with other communities ravaged by gun violence to launch March for Our Lives. Those brave teenagers with their unquenchable fire helped to deal a body blow to the gun lobby, convincing organizations to stop doing business with the National Rifle Association, and shaming politicians who accepted campaign contributions from the NRA. And yet Congress still refused to act. *Where is the outrage?* I wondered, my own anger a raging flame. *Don't they see that gun safety is about saving lives?* And that's when I decided: If Congress wouldn't join the fight, I would take the fight to Congress.

I filed to run from Georgia's Sixth Congressional District, where I lived, in the spring of 2018. For a black woman running as a gun-reform Democrat in a pro-gun, majority white district that had elected only white Republicans to the U.S. House since 1979, winning was a long shot. But that didn't stop me. Gun violence was an epidemic in our country, and it wasn't just poor people or minorities dying anymore. White people in suburbia were also losing loved ones. Sadly, for most people gun safety isn't an issue until it touches their own lives. It had been that way for me, too. But now I had a message to share, and it was simply this: No one should ever have to die from unnecessary gun violence. Our children shouldn't have to fear mass shooters. Teachers should feel safe in the classroom. Women shouldn't have to worry about a partner's gun in the drawer.

During my campaign, I knocked on doors, sat in living rooms, and spoke at town halls. And constituents heard me loud and clear because, well, none of them wanted to be me. But in a state where voter suppression was rampant, I took nothing for granted. On election night, November 6, 2018, as the ballots were being counted, the race was a toss-up between the incumbent Republican and me. That evening, I prayed with my husband Curtis, as I always did. "Lord," I said, "we've done everything you've asked of us, and now we give the outcome to you." We slept peacefully, and when we awoke I learned that I had won.

I entered Congress in a historic year, with more women and people of color elected to office than ever before. Going through orientation with the freshman members of the 116th Congress, I was exhilarated and overjoyed to be in a space that I had come to so many times before as a person seeking my elected officials' ear to listen to my cause, to hear my plea. Now, I got to be on the helping side. *God did that.*

As I write this in the summer of 2020, Americans from diverse walks of life are once again marching for racial justice and the sanctity of human life in numbers never before seen. And when my friend John Lewis succumbed to cancer on July 17, 2020, after representing Georgia's Fifth Congressional District for thirty-four years, the country mourned this giant of the civil rights movement and embraced his call to "redeem the soul of our nation." John Lewis understood that we must all be redeemers now, for there is still more work to do. And so, as one of God's emissaries, I will continue to go where I am directed with a faithful heart. *Standing Our Ground* tells the story of how my journey began, and how my love for Jordan points the way.

INTRODUCTION

In Guns We Trust

IN THAT DARKENED AUDITORIUM, I was one of a few brown faces among the mostly white evangelicals filling the seats around me. Not for the first time, I wondered why so few of the faith congregations I spoke to reflected the multihued family of God. I was in Columbia, South Carolina, for a screening of the award-winning documentary *The Armor of Light*. This deeply provocative film wrestles with theological questions of guns and faith, and features a pro-life white evangelical minister, and me, an African American mother grieving the loss of my only son to gun violence.

The Reverend Rob Schenck and I had been asked to participate in a panel discussion following the screening, along with Abigail Disney, the filmmaker who brought us together. As the opening credits rolled and a haunting score filled the theater, I silently asked God to speak through me that night, and to open my listeners' hearts to his message. Twenty-five minutes later, my body clenched against a fresh onslaught of pain as I watched myself on-screen: I was talking about my son, Jordan Russell Davis, who at seventeen had been fatally shot at a Jacksonville, Florida, gas station by a white man who thought the rap music he and his friends were playing on their car stereo was too loud.

As Jordan lay dying, the shooter drove away from the scene. We would soon discover that he was a licensed gun owner in the state of Florida, and a member of the National Rifle Association (NRA), which likely meant he took it as an article of Second Amendment faith that the blood he'd just spilled would soon be washed clean by a law called Stand Your Ground. He knew that under the statute, all he had to prove was that he *believed* the four black boys in the red Dodge Durango would do him harm. That claim alone gave him the right to use lethal force rather than to seek de-escalation and retreat.

There was no question my son's killer was versed in the particulars of this statute, and the way it could provide legal cover after the fact. The leadership of the NRA had assertively educated its members to drum up support for the law's inaugural passage in Florida in 2005. Versions of the legislation have since been adopted in twenty-three more states, leading in every case to a spike in deadly shootings. In Florida, for example, justifiable homicide cases tripled after the passage of Stand Your Ground, and in Georgia, they increased by 83 percent.[1]

The NRA's response to this increase was to offer up to $150,000 for criminal defense reimbursement, and up to one million dollars in liability protection should its members face legal reprisals after invoking the "shoot-first" law. And so, when arrested the next day, my son's killer immediately told police he'd felt threatened by Jordan and his friends. Despite the boys being unarmed, the shooter insisted he'd fired on them in self-defense.

I will never forget the way my breath left my body at the moment I grasped that the value of a black boy's life had been part of the shooter's split-second calculation *before* he reached for his gun. Suddenly, it was crystal clear to me what my son had been up against—a man who believed he could shoot to kill based on nothing more than a feeling, because he reckoned the state's gun law would absolve him in the death of an African American boy. No doubt he was rolling the dice that, if charged, his fate would lie in the hands of jurors who harbored the same deep-rooted biases and fears as he did—prejudices as old as America itself.

———

It was my opposition to the Stand Your Ground law that had led to my initial meeting, the one that would be filmed, with Rev. Rob Schenck. As chairman of the Evangelical Church Alliance, Rob had been unable to reconcile the pro-life stance of the Christian Right with its intense pro-gun fervor. He would eventually break with the evangelical leadership over its position on guns, but at the time we were making the film that hadn't happened yet. His theological struggle was the subject of our taped discussion as we'd sat in his rock-walled garden in the nation's capital and shared our respective encounters with gun violence.

Abigail Disney, founder of the feminist nonprofit Peace is Loud, kept the cameras rolling as we reflected on America's flawed gun policies, and the culture of fear and tribal antagonism that lobbyists for the nation's perilously lenient gun laws had cultivated. I could not help the tears as I observed to Rob that for so many Americans, guns had become a substitute for trust in God's protection. "As Christians, we have replaced God with our guns," I told him. "Instead of looking to God righteously, as the Protector, we're looking at our guns as the protector. And that's not the word of God."

My comment stunned the minister into silence, because he knew as well as I did that the largest and most zealous gun-owning demographic in America was his own flock—white evangelical Christians—along with less religious whites who held strong right-wing political views. They were, in a sense, "political evangelicals," unshakably committed to the party of Reagan.

Now, sitting with the reverend in a darkened theater in Columbia, South Carolina, I contemplated how one squared the commandment "Thou shalt not kill" with the readiness to take a human life. I weighed the ironies. Earlier, I had seen a man in a T-shirt emblazoned with the words "IN GUNS WE TRUST." I felt exactly the opposite. Surrendering my personal safety not to guns, but to God, felt like the ultimate security. Perhaps my own lack of fear had something to do with the fact that the very worst day of my life had already come and gone, and somehow, I was still standing. Even so, I believed my Heavenly Father would pro-tect me always, no matter the threats of death or sexual violence that I so often received as an advocate for commonsense gun laws—and despite the bullets that had pierced the flesh of my beloved child.

The United States is a notoriously gun-friendly culture, with more than 300 million firearms currently in circulation, almost one gun for every American man, woman, and child. Our country represents 5 percent of the world's population, yet we hold 50 percent of the world's guns. Our national passion for bearing arms was first en-coded in the twenty-seven words of the Second Amendment to the Constitution of the United States, set down in 1791 by the Founding Fathers at the birth of our frontier nation: "A well regulated Militia, being necessary to the security of a free State, the right of the people to keep and bear Arms, shall not be infringed."

While most gun safety advocates, myself included, have no quarrel with an individual's right to own a firearm, we would argue that, as written, the Second Amendment does not preclude the responsibility of the government to regulate how and by whom that gun might be purchased, discharged, carried, and stored for the protection of fellow citizens. Indeed, in the landmark *DC vs. Heller* decision of 2008, conservative Supreme Court justice Antonin Scalia held that "the Second Amendment right is not unlimited. It is not a right to keep and carry any weapon whatsoever in any manner whatsoever and for whatever purpose."[2]

To be clear: I completely understand owning a gun for sport or recreational purposes as well as for self-defense. I am not, and have never been, opposed to the Second Amendment. My own father was a hunter. I grew up in a household where there was always a licensed firearm, one that was stored and used with utmost respect and care. Even so, I question why so many white evangelicals, as well as non-churchgoing Christian whites, are now stockpiling military-grade assault weapons and high-capacity magazines expressly designed to wipe out scores of people quickly. Do they feel *that* unsafe? More to the point, doesn't our faith require that we put our trust in God to guard and defend us, rather than in our guns?

I have since come to understand that the attitudes that helped create a gun culture so dangerous to boys like mine, were bred in the hearts of citizens who profess their faith in God as fervently as they profess their right to bear arms. With the rise of the Christian Right as a political wave in the 1980s—one dedicated to preserving, among other values, the supremacy of whiteness—large swaths of America's evangelical population were coached by the profit-making agenda of the NRA to embrace fear and suspicion of anyone they saw as different from themselves, forsaking trust in God's protection and faith in the humanity of their fellow citizens.

These were some of the people I hoped to connect with in Columbia, South Carolina, that evening. I wanted to reach across America's cultural divide to open people's eyes to the epidemic of gun violence that has the nation in its cross hairs. I wanted that audience to understand that it isn't only boys like Jordan who are at risk; their sons and daughters are endangered, too, because whenever there is a gun in the midst of a conflict, no matter how minor or survivable the circumstance, too often someone ends up dead. In America, while individuals might discriminate based on deep-seated historical prejudices, firearms are ruthlessly egalitarian. People of every complexion fall victim to gun violence—a total of thirty-three thousand fatalities every year and ninety-six gun deaths *every single day*.

Among the dead are those spectacularly cut down in mass shootings at schools and churches, malls and movie theaters, workplaces and public parks. Less visible, but exponentially more numerous, are the women and other relatives murdered by domestic abusers who kept a gun in the bedside table drawer; heartsick teenagers who sucked on the barrel of a pistol; gang members acting out cruel grudges and initiations; children who accidentally discharged a weapon they believed was a toy. With so many guns in the possession of ordinary citizens, no one is immune. The scourge of violence cuts across all races, all ages and economic classes, all familial circumstances, affecting every corner of our society. Death by firearm can just as easily occur in poor, crime-ridden neighborhoods as in middle- and upper-income communities. We are, every one of us, trapped in this ongoing nightmare together. We have no choice but to stand together, and to stand our ground.

———

As the national spokesperson and faith and outreach leader for Everytown for Gun Safety and Moms Demand Action for Gun Sense in America, I've learned that one of the most effective tools in our arsenal is sharing our stories. The potency of personal experience is one reason that student survivors of the February 2018 school massacre in Parkland, Florida, were able to galvanize the nation with their calls for gun law reform. In much the same way that protesters had spilled onto the streets of Ferguson, Missouri, four years before, demanding an end to police violence against African American bodies, the survivors of the Parkland school shooting challenged us all, insisting we confront the failures of culture and government that allowed a troubled nineteen-year-old to mow down seventeen of their friends with a weapon of war.

I could cite numbers to show the enormity of the crisis we face, but in the end, it is our stories that will arouse people to step into the fray. By telling our stories, we shed light on the issues that define our lives; we become familiar and known to one another; and we create a space for other people to become engaged. Survivor stories like mine have helped convince 90 percent of Americans to support laws preventing the mentally ill from purchasing firearms, and fully three-quarters of the five million members of the NRA support universal background checks on all firearm sales. But their voices mean little to the organization's leadership. Guns in America are a deep, dark business, one that disguises its base capitalist motive by misdirecting our attention to issues of race, politics, and faith.

Beyond the smoke and mirrors, this book shows how the gun lobby won the allegiance of evangelicals in the 1980s, and traces how the Second Amendment came to symbolize freedom from government intrusion, even as NRA money put lawmakers in office who would loosen regulations beyond reason. The narrative also examines how the gun lobby enshrined whites' Second Amendment fervor by inciting fear of black and brown bodies; explores theological arguments surrounding the right to bear arms; and suggests how faith ministries can help redress the violence tearing our communities apart. But this is not a dry social analysis of America's gun culture. Rather, this book is the blood and guts of my life, the hard nights, and the unexpected brilliance of morning. It is the account of my son's short life and violent death, our family's search for justice, and my awakening to a call that will drive the rest of my days.

At its heart, this book is a mother's story—my way of making sure that my son's seventeen years on this earth will continue to have meaning. Perhaps the most extraordinary part of my journey has been watching my life be transformed in the wake of Jordan's death, being called out of the boat, stepping out on the water for a cause. Just as God did with Abraham, he said to me, *I am going to take you to a land where you've never been. You won't know anybody at first, you won't know how to do what I am asking of you, but I just need you to go. I will guide your steps.*

I know in every cell of my body that my son came into this world to make a difference, and in the end, he helped deliver me to my highest calling. His death showed me that I am to be a voice in the wilderness, joining a dynamic group of activists who are working to stem a red tide of violence, one fueled by the deadly interplay of guns, race, politics, and faith in American life. I have no doubt this is my divinely appointed purpose, but when tragedy arrived at my door in a sudden senseless burst of gunfire, I thought I had failed my child. I believed my life was over. And perhaps it was. But a new life opened up before me, and there was nothing else for me to do but claim it. In telling my story—and honoring the life of the child God entrusted to me—I am claiming it still.

PART ONE

THE PROMISE

CHAPTER 1

Black Friday

I THINK NOW THAT JORDAN himself called to me that evening.

It was the night after Thanksgiving, November 23, 2012. My husband, Curtis, and I were in Chicago, spending the weekend with my lifelong friend Terry and her husband, Earl. We had feasted on leftovers for dinner, and now the four of us were relaxing in the living room, watching television and chatting. I no longer recall what we talked about. I only know that at a few minutes before 10 PM, for no reason at all, I got up from my chair and walked upstairs to the bedroom in which Curtis and I had slept the night before.

"I'll be right back," I told the others. I'm sure they didn't give it a second thought. My own mind was a complete blank as I pushed open the bedroom door. Before any question as to why I was there could flicker into consciousness, I noticed that my phone, lying on the dresser, was buzzing and flashing the name "Ron Davis" on the screen. The ringer was off, so I would not have heard the phone from downstairs. I picked it up and answered my ex-husband's call.

"Hey Ron, how're you doing? You and Jordan have a good Thanksgiving?"

Almost two years before, our seventeen-year-old son, Jordan, had moved to Jacksonville, Florida, to finish out his high school years with his father. Jordan had lived with me in Atlanta ever since his dad and I divorced when he was four. But in the fall of 2010, when Jordan was fifteen and a tenth grader, I'd been diagnosed with breast cancer for a second time. I was facing surgery and radiation while Jordan and I were still getting used to being a refashioned family unit with my new husband, Curtis. Having beaten cancer once before, when Jordan was seven, I had full faith that I would once again recover. But as I underwent the rigors of radiation treatment, I worried about being able to give Jordan the attention he needed as a smart, energetic, and socially popular adolescent on the threshold of becoming a man. I made the tough call that it was time for him to go and live with his father.

Jordan opposed the idea at first. In fact, he was so angry with me for sending him away that he wouldn't take my phone calls for weeks. He'd always been an unabashed mama's boy, and the truth was, there was nothing in my life that I loved more than being Jordan's mother. But I felt sure he would grow from this time with his father, who was grateful to finally have a turn at raising our boy and showing him how to be a man.

Now I was healthy again, and by all accounts, Jordan was thriving in Jacksonville. But on the call that evening, Ron cleared his throat, and the hairs on my arms prickled. I sensed something ominous in his hesitation.

"Where are you?" he said finally.

"In Chicago, with Terry and Earl."

"I know," he said, "but where are you in the house?"

"In the bedroom." I paused. "Ron, what's wrong?"

"I need you to go and get Earl."

"Why? What's wrong?" I said, my voice rising.

On the other end of the line, Ron made a strangled sound, a cross between a moan and a sob. I think that was the moment when I *knew*. I felt suddenly hollowed out, a sick, sinking feeling at the center of my being, in the part of me where I had carried Jordan for nine long months and nurtured him to life.

"Where is Jordan?" I heard myself screaming. "What's wrong with Jordan?"

"Get Earl," Ron said again weakly, but I cut him off.

"I'm not getting Earl unless you tell me right now what is wrong with Jordan!"

"Jordan's at the hospital," Ron said. He spoke haltingly, as if he could barely summon the words. "He's been shot, Lucy. I need you to get on the first plane and come down here."

I sank down onto the side of the bed, my whole body shaking.

"Is my son alive?" I whispered.

Years would pass before I remembered Ron telling me that, no, Jordan had died. Our son, he said, had been out with his friends that evening when someone had taken his life. For a long time, I had no memory at all of Ron uttering those words, but I know he must have said them, because Terry told me later that she suddenly heard a piercing scream from the bedroom, and then I was running down the stairs, and everyone was running toward me, and I made it halfway down before I collapsed in a broken heap.

"Somebody shot my boy," I sobbed. "Jordan's been shot."

My voice was the sound of my heart ripping itself from my chest.

"Jordan is dead."

———

Terry and Curtis helped me down the stairs and onto the couch. Terry stayed by my side as the world swam before my eyes, dim and surreal. All I wanted was for Curtis to hold me until I woke from this nightmare. Because surely I would awaken soon—how long could this ordeal continue? But Curtis had become practical and businesslike. From somewhere in the room, I heard him on the phone with Delta Operations making arrangements for us to fly out in the morning. We were both longtime flight attendants with the airline, and that night the agents in Operations could not have been more kind. We had non-revved to Chicago (the industry term for non-revenue passengers who fill empty seats in a cabin), which usually meant traveling standby, but now the agents immediately issued emergency "Must Ride" passes for us back to Atlanta, and then on to Jacksonville.

After Curtis put down the phone, he went upstairs to pack our things. An eerie silence settled over Terry and Earl's house. It was as if the entire world had gone still, and in one small corner of it I sat huddled with my arms wrapped around myself, weeping and rocking, weeping and rocking. Terry was sobbing, too. It was the first time in all the decades I'd known her that I'd ever seen her cry. Despite his efficient activity, Curtis was also in tears, and so was Earl, who seemed angry and bewildered. He paced up and down the house, his fists balled against his sides. "Not Jordan," he kept saying. "How could this happen?"

It slowly dawned on me that I needed to let others who loved Jordan know he had been taken from us. I roused myself enough to call my sister, Lori, out in San Diego. She had been like a second mother to Jordan. We always spent Christmas and the month of July at her home in California. Her three children and Jordan had grown up as bonded as siblings.

"Oh my Lord, who shot Jordan?" Lori wailed in disbelief.

I told her I didn't know.

Later, people would say: Didn't you want to call Ron back and get more details? Didn't you want to know how everything had unfolded, and who took the life of your child? Looking back, I can see that none of it really mattered that night. The only thing that counted, the only truth I knew, was that I would never again hold my son's physical body close. I would never again feel the warmth of him, or rest my gaze on the particular shade of brown of his skin, or bask in the light that danced in his eyes as he bent to kiss my forehead before heading out of the house with his friends.

"Peace out, Mom," he would call, holding up two fingers as he shrugged into his favorite brown hoodie and stepped into his red Vans sneakers. All night, this vision of Jordan was all I could see—my son, vibrantly alive.

———

Ron and his wife, Carolina, met us at the Jacksonville airport. We hugged each other solemnly and hardly spoke. The forty-minute car ride back to the house was thick with sorrow. My robotic numbness only hinted at my state of shock. By this time, Jordan's death was all over the news, so we knew that a white middle-aged man had pumped ten bullets into the SUV in which my son and his three friends were sitting. Mercifully, the other boys escaped physical injury, but three of the bullets had found their mark in my boy. I still didn't know why he had been shot or if his killer had been taken into custody, but I was determined to wait until we got to Ron's house to ask questions, because once we started talking, I would surely fall apart.

But we did everything right.

The thought ticked in my brain like a metronome. How could a volley of bullets from a man completely unknown to us have taken the life of my only son? We'd raised Jordan in a protected environment. He'd always lived in a nice house on a quiet residential street, and he went to church every week. God was at the center of our lives and we had loving relationships with family members and friends. When I'd sent Jordan to Jacksonville, it was only so that his father could watch over him. Like me, Ron had monitored his friends, made sure there was no unlawful activity around our boy, and never any threat of violence in the gated middle-class community where they lived. His friends were decent kids on the verge of graduating high school. Most of them planned to go on to college, while Jordan, who excelled in ROTC, had been talking about joining the Marines. Mentally, emotionally, and spiritually, he had been in a good place.

When I'd last spoken with my son on Thanksgiving morning, he'd told me he planned to go shopping with his friends on Black Friday. He was excited because his girlfriend, Aliyah, worked at Urban Outfitters in the mall, and he'd get to see her. A few weeks before, she'd been disappointed when he refused to bring the flowers he'd got for her birthday to school. Jordan hadn't wanted to deal with the other kids teasing him, but now he couldn't wait to see his girl and make it up to her. His dad had given him some money, and he planned to get her a Christmas present. We'd tossed around some gift ideas before hanging up the phone.

"I love you, son," I'd signed off the call.

"Love you, too, Ma," he'd said.

At least my boy got to experience being in love, I thought as we passed small white sailboats bobbing in the distance of the St. Johns River, which ran for a stretch along the highway. The river was the same gunmetal gray as the sky, the same bleak gray as the world without my son. I had the strange sensation that I was floating alone on a gray overcast sea, as aimless as those boats. I reached across the back seat and grasped Curtis's hand, hoping it would anchor me.

———

Throughout the morning, Ron gave us the details he'd learned from the police, and from the boys who had been in the car with Jordan. Two of them—Leland Brunson and Tevin Thompson—had come by with Leland's parents to offer condolences to Ron and Carolina the day before. No one could understand how Jordan had ended up dead. "Jordan was my third son; I loved that boy," Leland's mother, Tanya Booth-Brunson, said later. "He had this shine on him that lit up the room. He was a star, and everyone knew it."

Ron told me Leland had sat for a long time in Jordan's room, crying inconsolably. He was skinny and small for his seventeen years, and he had been Jordan's best friend ever since our son moved to Jacksonville. Tevin was a big guy compared to Leland. He was also seventeen, with a round face and a megawatt smile, but it was nowhere in evidence that day.

The third young man, Tommie Stornes, had driven the boys to the mall in his red Dodge Durango that Black Friday afternoon. Tommie, two years older than the others, was lean and somber-eyed, with shoulder-length dreadlocks. Ron didn't know him as well as the other two boys; he and Jordan had met through mutual friends only a couple of months before. But Tommie was unfailingly polite, which Ron appreciated.

At the Town Center mall, Jordan had hung out with Aliyah while the other boys chatted up girls they knew. On their way to another mall, they cranked the music up loud in Tommie's car, all of them rapping along and having a good time. The boys wanted gum and

Tommie wanted Newports, so he turned the SUV into the Gate Gas Station at the corner of Southside Boulevard and Baymeadows Road. He pulled into a parking spot in front of the convenience store at nearly 7:30 PM. There were no cars on either side of him. As he shut off the engine, the song "Beef" by rapper Lil Reese came on the radio. Tommie was moving his shoulders to the beat as he went into the store.

A few minutes later, a car pulled into the parking spot on the passenger side of the Durango. A brown-haired woman got out and entered the store. The driver, a barrel-chested white man with iron-gray hair, who looked to be in his late forties, rolled down his window and told the boys to turn the music down. Tevin reached over and turned down the volume, but from the back seat, Jordan told him to turn the music back up. Tevin later speculated that Jordan didn't like the way the man had spoken to them. They exchanged words. Tommie was completely unaware of the conflict between the man and Jordan as he danced his way back to the car. But as he slid into the driver's seat and switched on the ignition, he suddenly saw the man in the vehicle next to them aiming a pistol their way.

Pop! Pop! Pop!

Pop! Pop! Pop! Pop!

The shots kept coming.

Wild with panic, Tommie threw the car into reverse, floored the gas pedal, and backed away from the gunfire as fast as he could. The man kept shooting at them. He even got out of his car and crouched so he could aim better. Tommie executed a frantic two-point turn and raced toward an adjacent parking lot. When he couldn't hear the sound of gunfire anymore, he stopped the vehicle.

He jumped out of the car, breathing hard.

"Everybody okay?" he asked.

He called each of his friends by name. Jordan was the only one who didn't respond. There was a gurgling sound coming from his throat, as if he was gasping for air. Leland reached around and patted Jordan down to see where he was hurt. When his hands touched the warm, sticky wetness spreading across Jordan's chest, Leland wrapped both arms around his friend and held him as he died.

———

At around 9 PM, Ron got the call from Leland's mother. Tanya told him Tommie's car had been shot at in the parking lot of the Gate Gas Station, and that Leland, Tommie, and Tevin were downtown at the Police Memorial Building giving statements. She was headed there now.

"Where's Jordan?" Ron asked her.

"All I know is Jordan is at Shands Hospital," Tanya told him. "The other boys are okay, but Jordan—" she faltered. "Ron, Jordan took a bullet."

Ron ran to his car and raced to the hospital. He burst into the ER, heart pounding, demanding to see his son. At first the nurses wouldn't give him any information because they couldn't be sure who he was. He was a tall, agitated African American man with no identification; he'd rushed out of the house grabbing only his phone and his keys. Finally, he showed them a photo of Jordan on his phone to convince them he was his father. That's when they took him into a room, and called the doctor and the chaplain. The two men sat him down and told him that his son was dead, and they needed him to identify the body. They explained that three bullets had pierced Jordan's pelvis, lungs, and aorta, and they asked him not to touch his body, as there was an active police investigation and they didn't want him to disturb any evidence. But as soon as Ron saw Jordan lying there on the stretcher, he collapsed over him, cradling his head in one palm, kissing his face, his tears soaking the sheet that covered his son's mortal wounds.

"Jordan looked like he was sleeping," Ron told me as we sat in his living room. He stared down at his large hands. I knew he was remembering the last time those hands would ever touch our son. "I swear Lucy, he looked as peaceful as an angel."

He said the chaplain had prayed over Jordan's body, and that was comforting to me. I suddenly remembered a night several months before, on one of Jordan's visits back home to Atlanta. He had told me, seemingly out of the blue, "Mom, I'm not afraid to die, because when my time comes, I know where I'm going."

He'd been perched on a stool at the kitchen counter, watching me stuff manicotti shells with ricotta cheese. "That's right, son," I had answered, smiling as I layered the manicotti in a casserole dish. "You'll be with your Heavenly Father."

It was only then that the strangeness of my strong, athletic boy contemplating his own death occurred to me, and I understood my son's comment to be something more than a declaration of his faith.

Earlier that week, we'd talked about Trayvon Martin, an African American boy the same age as Jordan, who'd been shot and killed in Sanford, Florida, several months before. A neighborhood watch captain had pursued the unarmed teen while he was walking home from the store, his hoodie pulled up against the rain. I realized Jordan was weighing the fact that being profiled to death was a possibility more real for him than for his white peers—because we both knew that if Trayvon had been a white teenager walking home from the store that night, he would still be alive.

"You know, Jordan," I said, "as a young black man you will meet people in life who do not value you. But never forget that God values you, and I value you, and you must value yourself. I truly believe you are here to do God's work, and"—I winked at him as I stirred tomato sauce to pour over the manicotti—"you better marry and give me grandchildren."

Jordan didn't laugh as I'd expected he might. Instead he was silent for a few moments, shoulders hunched, elbows on the counter, his brow knitted in thought. Then he sighed. "I'm just saying, Ma, you never know. But I'm not afraid."

And now, in the blink of an eye, in the pull of a trigger, he was gone. I shivered to think that somewhere in his spirit, Jordan had seen that his life with us would be cut short. Could God have shown him that his time was at hand—because what seventeen-year-old contemplates his own death while his mama is making his favorite meal on an ordinary summer evening?

———

I didn't see my son's body until his memorial service at Giddens Funeral Home three days later. A larger service of thanksgiving for his life was planned for the following Friday, to be held at Trinity Chapel back home in Atlanta, but Ron and I wanted Jordan's friends in Jacksonville to have an opportunity to say goodbye. I stood beside my boy's open casket, undone by the stillness of death. This was my child's body, so handsome in dark pants, a crisp white shirt, and blue tie, but it was clear to me that his animating spirit was elsewhere. As I'd requested, Jordan's left hand was curled around a ceramic figurine I'd given him the Christmas before, a small boy with a big red heart on his chest, bearing the words "You'll always have my heart." His right hand rested on the much-used Bible he kept in his bedside table drawer. I touched the Bible and tried to imagine my son safe in the embrace of his Heavenly Father and loved ones on the other side.

Suddenly, there was a stir of whispers in the chapel. Everyone looked toward the door as three beautiful young women entered the sanctuary. Two of the girls were comforting the one in the middle, who was crying, and I realized this must be Aliyah, the girl Jordan had talked to me about. She paused a few feet away from me, her eyes meeting mine uncertainly. I saw that she was unsure how to approach me, so I went to her and took her hands in mine, and thanked her for being there for Jordan. Tears sat on her eyelashes as she looked into my eyes with such pity and regret. "I'm so sorry," she mumbled. It stunned me to see my grief reflected in the eyes of one so young. Her sorrow made my own more real, but I tried to push it down. I wasn't ready yet to relinquish the delusion that this was all a nightmare from which I would soon awaken.

That entire afternoon was a blur for me, my sense of unreality compounded by the fact that I knew hardly any of the people in the small chapel, weeping over my son. I was an outsider there, at my own child's memorial service. And while I was grateful to see that my son had been warmly embraced in his father's hometown, I couldn't wait to bring his body back to my own faith congregation at Trinity, and to the village of people who had helped me raise him in Atlanta, his first home.

———

By Monday, we knew who had shot Jordan. A homeless man living out of his car had witnessed the entire incident and had jotted down the license plate of the shooter's vehicle as he left the scene. We would learn that the man who killed Jordan was Michael Dunn, a forty-five-year-old software developer and gun collector from Satellite Beach, Florida. He had traveled to Jacksonville with his fiancée, Rhonda Rouer, to attend his son's wedding that afternoon. On the way back to their hotel, they'd stopped at the Gate Gas Station because Rouer wanted to pick up a bottle of wine and some chips. She'd heard the gunshots from inside the store, and when she got back to the car Dunn yelled for her to get in.

"I just fired at those kids," he told her as he peeled out of the parking lot.

The next morning, Rouer saw on the news that one of the kids from the previous night's shooting had died. Upset, she insisted she and Dunn leave Jacksonville immediately and return home. Police arrested Dunn at his residence in Satellite Beach later that day. They charged him with one count of first-degree murder and three counts of attempted murder.

It was our attorney, John Phillips, who briefed us on all this. He'd driven out to Ron's home on Monday afternoon to meet Curtis and me, and to update us on the status of the investigation. A friend of Ron's, a newscaster in the Jacksonville area, had referred John to us. We trusted him immediately. He was compassionate but plainspoken as he outlined the details of the case so far. He reported that Michael Dunn would plead not guilty at his arraignment later that week, and he warned that Dunn's attorneys would most likely invoke Florida's Stand Your Ground law, arguing that their client feared for his life and had fired at the boys in self-defense.

And there it was—the inevitable calculus of race in the violent encounter that had ended the life of my son.

Michael Dunn was white.

Jordan and his friends were black.

And now my son's killer was claiming he had fired ten bullets into the boys' vehicle because he'd believed he was in imminent danger. In statements made through his lawyer, Dunn insisted the boys had threatened his life, and that he'd seen Jordan point a gun at him. Or maybe it was a metal pipe. Except we knew there had been no threat, just as there were never any weapons in that car of good and loved young men.

In his law office a few days later, John Phillips was meticulous in helping us understand the hurdles we would face as we pursued justice for Jordan. He explained that Stand Your Ground was based on the castle doctrine in English common law, which gave homeowners the right to forcefully defend their homes and property from a perceived threat without the requirement to retreat. Stand Your Ground essentially extended the concept of defending one's castle to include one's physical body, giving individuals who felt endangered the right to shoot to kill and ask questions later.

The tricky thing about the law, John reminded us, was that the threat didn't have to be real. Michael Dunn merely had to claim the *perception* that he was in danger in order to seek the shelter of Stand Your Ground. If my son's killer could convince a jury that four young black men had mortally terrified him, he would walk away from his crime. Indeed, in the twenty-four states where Stand Your Ground had already been adopted, 70 percent of those who sought its cover avoided legal punishment. Worse, in cases where the shooter was white and the victim black, criminal charges were seldom filed at all. And when such cases *were* brought before the court, a white defendant charged with shooting a black victim in self-defense was eleven times more likely to be acquitted than in cases where the defendant was black and the victim white.

I recalled bitterly the words on a handmade sign I'd seen at a rally protesting Trayvon Martin's death. Like Michael Dunn, Trayvon's killer had invoked the protection of Stand Your Ground. As the case wound its way through Florida's criminal justice system, the country had become painfully familiar with the doctrine. Gun safety advocates and Second Amendment proponents were increasingly polarized over Stand Your Ground, and the deadly way it so often intersected with race. Across the country, people marched to proclaim that black lives mattered. At one of those marches, the sign that a young woman held high perfectly summed up for me the trouble with the Stand Your Ground law: "When my skin is the weapon you fear, I can never be unarmed."

The truth of those words cut through me now, because I understood that Michael Dunn would insist he'd been confronted by a car full of "thugs" that evening. He'd commented as much to his fiancée before she went into the convenience store. "I hate that thug music," she would later report him saying. He could not see that my tender child was no thug, and neither were his friends. They were just teenagers out having a good time, young men looking to the future, one of them already finished high school and the other three just months away from walking across the stage for their diplomas.

My whole body slumped in my chair as the full reality of my son's murder hit me squarely in the chest. *God show me what to do now*, I beseeched my Lord. My child was dead. My whole purpose for waking up each morning had been torn away. How would I go on? Where would I find meaning? I had no clue. I begged God for an answer, my desolation at last absolute.

What I didn't yet understand was that my years of parenting Jordan were not over. As his mother, I still had work to do, because just as my son's spirit had called me upstairs on the night of Black Friday, he had left me a charge to move forward in the very manner of his death. But I couldn't see it yet. I was too lost in grief and anguish to realize that through Jordan, I was already being guided to a purpose greater than any I could have dreamed for myself. It was a call to action that I would come to understand had been mine all along. God had begun planting the seeds right from the beginning, starting with the family into which I had been born.

CHAPTER 2

Civil Rights Baby

A BURST OF LIGHT HIT the corner of my eye, and then our whole house shook with the rumble of crashing glass. I clutched the blue wax crayon I was using to color a lake scene and crept out to our enclosed front porch. Standing to one side of the window, I saw at once where the blast had happened: across the street, thick flames licked skyward from the shattered glass front of Mr. K's Grocery Store. In front of it, a knot of teenage boys yelled and waved their fists at the flames; one threw stones into the fire's red maw. I couldn't hear their shouts over the roar of the flames, but I could see they were angry; thick veins stood out in their necks; their mouths were howling circles of rage, their eyes blazed as hot as the fire. And they were not alone. People were racing up and down our street, kicking over trash cans, throwing rocks, cans, bottles, everybody yelling.

It was the morning of April 5, 1968. In two months, I would turn eight years old. I'd lived with my parents and younger sister, Lori, on that street in Joliet, Illinois, for going on three years. Usually, South Chicago Street was calm and neighborly, with Lori and me dashing in and out of our friends' homes, playing jump rope in the alley next to our redbrick bungalow or hide-and-seek in the back yard. Sometimes, we'd kick off our shoes and dance to the Motown hits that blared from two huge speakers in front of Mr. Dunn's Record Store. Mr. Dunn was directly to our right. I noticed now that his storefront wasn't broken like Mr. K's, even though one of his speakers had been knocked on its side and was lying in the street. That didn't stop the Queen of Soul Aretha Franklin from belting out a gutsy rendition of her latest single:

> R-E-S-P-E-C-T
> *Find out what it means to me*

Aretha's rousing soundtrack cut through the smoky air, making the scene outside even stranger. I couldn't understand any of it. My neighbors just didn't behave this way. At the far edge of my mind, I wondered: Did Mr. K's store get firebombed and Mr. Dunn's didn't because Mr. K was a white in the black part of town, while Mr. Dunn was African American and lived right there in the neighborhood with the rest of us? Not that this sort of thing had ever mattered before, at least not as far as I could tell. We all shopped up and down South Chicago Street, paying no mind to the color of the shopkeeper. Why would today be any different? And yet, I sensed it *was* different.

Now I noticed a tall white man in khaki standing at the foot of the steps leading up to our porch. A green helmet cast the top half of his face in shadow, and one hand was curled around the long rifle slung over his shoulder. He stood straight and still as a statue, with only his eyes roving, taking in the rioters in the street, some carting boxes from ransacked stores. Like the boys yelling in front of Mr. K's, the rioters' bodies were contortions of rage—and something else, some other emotion I couldn't place back then.

Much later, I would recognize the look I'd seen on the rioters' faces. I would understand that their hearts had been broken, and what I was reading in every line of their bodies was a volatile mix of sorrow, desperation, rebellion, and fear. But I was still years away from grasping just how betrayed black America was feeling that day. I only knew that the violence outside my window frightened me. I made myself small behind the curtain, watching the chaos, trying to figure out what had set people off.

"Little Lou, come away from the window right now!" my mother, Wilma, shouted from the kitchen. She came to the front door and quickly pulled me inside by the hand, away from the sound of a fire truck screaming toward Mr. K's Grocery. "Stay in the back with Lori," she commanded, her hands on my shoulders, steering me. "It's too dangerous out here."

I peered up at my mother's face, and saw that her eyes were red and puffy. She had been crying. Even at seven years old, I was so connected to her that I absorbed the full weight of her sadness. Something had gone horribly wrong. A sense of dread hung in the air as if, inside our house, life as we knew it had come to a mournful halt. But I stopped myself from asking my mother what had happened. It seemed too big, and I wasn't ready to know. Instead, I joined my sister in the bedroom we shared. Lori was four years old. She looked up at me curiously as I threw myself across my bed, then she went back to dressing her Barbie. As my little sister played, I lay staring at the ceiling and listening as hard as I could to what our mother was saying on the phone.

"Yes, Lucien, yes, they sent the National Guard," I heard her tell my father. "He's out there now. No, they're still burning the place down. When will you be home?"

And later, on another call: "Oh dear God, Kathleen, I was afraid this would happen. I think he saw it, too."

Sometime in the afternoon, when I heard the television go on in the family room, I left Lori to play alone and went to find our mother. She barely noticed me as I settled myself next to her on the sofa. On the television, a news anchor was talking about Dr. Martin Luther King Jr. as pictures of him filled the screen, photographs from every stage of his thirty-nine years of life. Mom and I listened as the newscaster described how a sniper's bullet had pierced the civil rights leader's jaw and severed his spinal cord while he stood on a balcony of the Lorraine Motel in Memphis, Tennessee, the evening before. The shots rang out at just after 6 PM on April 4, 1968. I looked over at Mom, taking in her weariness, her lonely sorrow. It was only then that I understood that the great man had been gunned down.

Dr. King was dead.

I knew who Dr. King was. He was our prince of peace; a relentless advocate for nonviolent resistance to racial and economic injustice; the activist preacher whose courage inspired and informed the regular meetings Daddy convened in our home.

My father, Lucien, had left home early that morning. I'd assumed he'd gone to his office, but now I wondered if maybe he was out somewhere dealing with this news. It dawned on me that the National Guardsman had been stationed at the foot of our steps, protecting our family, because Daddy was an important man in our town. He was Joliet's only black dentist, and that conferred a certain privilege on Lori and me—everybody knew us as "Doc Holman's girls." But I was sure it was Daddy's other role as president of the Illinois chapter of the National Association for the Advancement of Colored People—the NAACP—that had caused a soldier to be stationed in front of our house. I guessed it was also the reason our phone didn't stop ringing all day.

Daddy arrived home toward nightfall, his '67 lavender Chrysler steering a careful path through the overturned trash cans and still-burning debris on South Chicago Street. I heard the distinctive sound of his engine as he turned into the driveway, and I tiptoed back out to the front porch to wait for him. I saw that the worst of the rioting and looting had died down, and the fire in Mr. K's store had been extinguished, leaving twisted steel and charred wood silhouetted against a setting sky. On the street, people stood and talked in clusters. Some sat on the edge of the sidewalk, faces buried in their hands. Daddy patted my head distractedly as he came through the door, shrugging off his gray suit coat and loosening his tie. I followed him into the family room, where my mom still sat transfixed by what was unfolding on our television—footage of riots and looting in other cities, and a local reporter estimating Joliet's damage in excess of one million dollars. While Mommy was sad, Daddy seemed angry, and I resolved to keep out of his way.

On the news, Dr. King's final sermon from the day before his death played on a seemingly endless loop: "We've got some difficult days ahead," he had told an overflow crowd at the Mason Temple in Memphis. "But it really doesn't matter with me now, because I've been to the mountaintop . . . And I've looked over, and I've seen the Promised Land. I may not get there with you. But I want you to know tonight that we, as a people, will get to the Promised Land."

His booming cadence, the hypnotic rise and fall of his voice, the far-seeing look in his eyes, all of it gave me chills. And now Mom was crying again, the tears flowing unchecked. Daddy sat hunched over, rubbing his temples, eyes closed, a bristling intensity about him. Suddenly it all made sense: The people who gathered around our dining table to plan marches and boycotts were all part of Dr. King's righteous army. *I* was part of his army. From the time we could walk, my sister and I had marched alongside our parents in the baking sun. Our mother held our hands tight as our father led a long column of protesters shouting about justice and equality and singing "We Shall Overcome." My parents, Lori, and me, all the people we marched with, we were fighting for the same cause as Dr. King—black people's full recognition as equal citizens under the law, with all the rights and privileges that our nation had long accorded to white people.

Even before I understood what they were about, I'd always loved the preparation for those marches—those evenings when Daddy presided over the kitchen table meetings, the lively debates, loud voices punctuated by bursts of laughter, the air thick with cigarette smoke, the latest hits from Motown playing on the radio. Some evenings, people would spread out into the living room with markers and poster board, creating signs to be carried at the protests. I think now that I relished those meetings because Daddy was always so central to them, so energetically present, a larger-than-life figure who, if truth be told, I usually watched from the sidelines.

On non-meeting nights, Daddy would disappear downstairs, typing and cutting and pasting for hours to assemble the latest issue of his monthly NAACP newspaper, *The Voice*. Lori and I knew not to disturb him as he worked, the basement completely dark but for the light over his drafting desk, and the glow of the Coca-Cola machine in one corner. The clink of another bottle of Coke falling into the slot was a comforting sound in those days. It meant Daddy was home, sipping his favorite soda pop and working diligently on his articles, and everything was predictable and normal. It also meant that in a few days, our mother would bundle the newspapers with rope cord and place the stacks carefully on the front seat of our car. Then she'd wrap Lori and me in blankets and tuck us into the back seat. She would settle us on pillows and give us our coloring books and favorite dolls, all to keep us occupied as she drove all over the state to deliver the newest issue of *The Voice*.

Even as a small child, I knew my parents were engaged in important work in the interest of this country, in something called *the movement*. But now, on the night after Dr. King was assassinated, and my people had taken to the streets, I grasped for the first time that my father's activism was not only urgent, but also dangerous. It had gotten Dr. King killed.

———

I find it curious now that my first vivid childhood memory is of a black man cut down in an unspeakable act of gun violence. The tentative connections I began to make on that day would foreshadow my future, both the tragedy that awaited me, and the activism it would provoke. In a very real sense, I was aware of the destructive power of firearms from the start, even though it would be decades before I embraced the fight for gun safety as my personal charge.

In terms of public awareness of the need for tougher gun regulations, 1968 was a wake-up call for the entire nation. Only two months after Dr. King was shot, Senator Robert F. Kennedy, the leading Democratic candidate for president, was gunned down in Los Angeles' Ambassador Hotel ballroom right after winning the California primary. These two killings, along with the earlier assassinations of President John F. Kennedy and civil rights leader Medgar Evers, both in 1963, convinced then-president Lyndon B. Johnson that firearms had to be more rigorously legislated. He proposed that every gun sale be registered in a national database, and every gun owner be licensed, but that bill was defeated in Congress. Legislators did pass a watered-down version, which became known as the Gun Control Act of 1968. It merely restricted the sale of guns by mail order, a nod to the fact that the weapon used to kill President Kennedy had been acquired through the US mail. Johnson was not pleased. "If guns are to be kept out of the hands of the criminal, out of the hands of the insane, and out of the hands of the irresponsible, then we must have licensing," he reiterated as he signed the woefully inadequate Gun Control Act into law. "The voices that blocked these safeguards were not the voices of an aroused nation. They were the voices of a powerful lobby, a gun lobby."[1]

The gun lobby had a name: the National Rifle Association. The group had been founded in 1871 to provide training in marksmanship for hunters and recreational shooters. However, after President Johnson's push to regulate gun sales, the organization would harden its opposition to any legislative oversight of guns at all.

Prior to 1968, there had been only two federal gun laws on the books, both of them passed in the 1930s. One was aimed at limiting gangland killings by imposing a tax on machine guns, and the other regulated the sale of firearms across state lines. For the next three decades, meaningful gun law reform tended to happen only on the state level, in response to local events. In California in 1967, for example, when members of the Black Panther Party for Self-Defense marched on the State Capitol in a conspicuous demonstration of their right to openly bear arms, then-governor Ronald Reagan threw his support behind a bill banning open carry, a law that remains on the books in California to this day. At the time, Reagan declared that he saw "no reason why on the street today a citizen should be carrying loaded weapons." He added that guns were a "ridiculous way to solve problems that have to be solved among people of good will," and that banning the open carry of firearms "would work no hardship on the honest citizen."[2]

I could not agree more with these statements, though it is not lost on me that only when a group of black men asserted their equal right to openly bear arms did legislators move to block the presence of guns in public places. A further irony is the fact that, after winning the White House in 1980, Reagan would become the NRA's most powerfully placed ally, now arguing for looser gun regulations. Despite an assassination attempt on his life in 1981, Reagan and the NRA forged a close bond during his presidency. A conservative Republican, he was the first candidate to ride into the Oval Office on a campaign machine robustly funded by the increasingly militant gun lobby. The president returned the favor by lavishing praise on the NRA's initiatives and delivering the keynote at their 1983 national meeting. "Locking them up, the hard-core criminals, and throwing away the key is the best gun-control law we could ever have," Reagan boomed from the podium. "We will never disarm any American who seeks to protect his or her family from fear and harm."[3]

This comment by no less than the president of the United States slipped right into the narrative long promoted by the leadership of the NRA, one in which urban black and brown people were equated with criminality and rural conservative whites were lauded as the "good Americans" who had every right under the Second Amendment to defend their "castles" with lethal force. It's an attitude that harks all the way back to early colonial settlers, who deployed armed militias against indigenous people, taking over their lands, and constituted armed slave patrols to ensure the protection of southern white plantation owners against black revolt. At one point, African American men were specifically restricted from owning guns through the Black Codes and Jim Crow laws. Later, during the 1960s, black gun owners formed their own organizations to protect communities of color from state violence. One such group was the Black Panther Party, which as governor of California Reagan had sought to weaken through his now-ironic ban on the open carry of firearms.

A decade later, as Reagan courted white evangelical voters, winning their allegiance with his pro-life platform and promise to overturn *Roe vs. Wade*, the right to bear arms became an equally loud rallying cry among Christian conservatives. Inflamed by racial dog whistles from right-wing candidates touting the preservation of American family values, white Christian evangelicals flocked to the Republican Party, amassing political clout under the banners of the Second Amendment and the pro-life movement, two arguably contradictory ideals.

It would take another ten years before gun reform advocates posted any significant victory in the battle for stricter federal legislation. In 1993, Democratic president Bill Clinton signed into law the Brady Bill, which instituted a five-day waiting period for required background checks on gun buyers. A year later, Clinton successfully pushed to ban assault weapons as part of his crime bill; unfortunately, the ban would expire in 2004. But the political fallout of the ban would last way beyond its expiration: After the passage of the 1994 crime bill, the NRA—which had formerly been bipartisan in its campaign contributions, with one third of its funding going to Democratic races—now threw almost 100 percent of the organization's financial support to Republicans, calculating that the party's rightward shift meant its candidates were more closely allied with the gun lobby's aims. Indeed, Republican legislators whose campaigns had been heavily leveraged by the deep-pocketed NRA would vote to weaken the background check provision by shortening the required waiting period.

The alliance between right-wing politics, Christian evangelism, and gun lobby money had long put firearm safety advocates in a bind, especially after former Border Patrol agent Harlon Carter became executive vice president of the NRA in 1977, and began steering the organization in a more aggressively pro-gun direction. Carter opposed background checks of any stripe, and asserted that the acquisition of firearms by violent felons and the mentally ill was simply the price of freedom. "No politician in America, mindful of his political career, would want to challenge our legitimate goals,"[4] he warned, and legislators, beholden to the realities of campaign fundraising and right-wing voter pandering, fell in line, setting the stage for what has become our most destructive political trope: elected officials who consider the gun lobby too wealthy and too powerfully connected to antagonize. And so they take the path of least resistance, sleepwalking in lockstep with the NRA's profit-driven aims.

For a long time, I was mostly unconscious, too. It would take me decades to wake from my own slumber, and to understand that confronting the radical agenda of the NRA was perhaps the most urgent civil rights issue of our time. Belatedly, I would grasp that for communities of color in particular, the proliferation of firearms has been devastating, with black children ten times more likely to die from gun violence than white children.[5] Yet politicians bought and paid for by the gun lobby seem to view the destruction of black bodies as just so much collateral damage, a wholly acceptable trade-off for Second Amendment freedoms. This indifference to the survival of our communities, so deeply rooted in our nation's history, is what makes the fight for gun law reform absolutely critical to the preservation of African American lives.

———

Even though I studied political science at Virginia State University in Petersburg after high school, and interned with state senator Douglas Wilder during the spring semester of my junior year, it never occurred to me that my future would be in advocacy, not even when Daddy arranged for me to intern as a legislative aide with the DC branch of the NAACP one summer. My role was to track legislation pertaining to minorities, including voter registration and civil rights. I did get a thrill being on Capitol Hill. It felt like my natural habitat, and I flirted with the idea of going to law school. But after graduating college in 1982, I fell into a data-collection job in Columbia, Maryland, and was bored to tears. Serendipitously, walking by a job board one day, I saw that Delta Airlines was hiring. Seduced by the idea of traveling the world, I applied to become a flight attendant. I told myself I would fly for a year and then go to law school.

Four years later, I was still with the airline. I found I loved flying, the camaraderie of crew members, always being on the go. I enjoyed experiencing different cultures and people, and trying unfamiliar foods. Mine wasn't the kind of job where you went to work and did the same thing day after day. Every assignment was something new, somewhere new, the promise of adventure—I loved that.

Daddy wasn't too pleased that I'd cast my lot with Delta. He had loftier aspirations for his daughter, and was sorely disappointed that I hadn't followed through with my original plan to study law. It didn't help his opinion of my career choice that my new employer was based in Atlanta, in the cradle of what had once been the Jim Crow South. Daddy was a race man through and through. He wasn't going to be happy with any work I chose unless it had to do with uplifting our people.

Growing up, I'd heard him say again and again: "Looky here, Lulu, you've got to fight for what you believe in, every damn thing, every damn day. You've got to fight for what you want, you've got to fight for what you deserve, because some people, they don't want you to have a damn thing." Daddy's passion for affirming the race extended well beyond what most people would imagine to be a mark of black pride. I'll never forget the Christmas when he arrived home with a black-flocked tree, gleeful at his find. "Now *that* is a Black Power tree!" he crowed as he pulled out the holiday decorations and set about dressing our charcoal-colored tree. My mother thought it was the ugliest Christmas tree she'd ever seen—who ever heard of a pine tree sprayed completely black? But no one could convince Daddy that our tree wasn't the height of black consciousness.

And yet, when it came to race relations, Lori and I were extremely sheltered children. Within our solid middle-class existence, my mother had created for Doc Holman's girls an idyll of afternoons at the local swimming pool, gymnastics and ballet classes, tap dancing and violin lessons, and picnics in the park with our friends. Occasionally on Sunday, my mother took us to the Lutheran house of worship, the only one in Joliet. She had been raised in the Lutheran church in Buffalo, New York, and it was where she felt most at home spiritually. But among the Lutheran congregation in Joliet, we were usually the only black family in the pews. Perhaps that accounts for why we went to church mostly on high holy days, like Good Friday, Easter, and Christmas. My mother was a devout Christian woman, and she taught us to say our prayers nightly before bed, but we attended church only sporadically.

Even though Wilma held a bachelor's degree in nursing, during those years on South Chicago Street, she was a busy stay-at-home mom. She saw not just to our social graces, but also to our academic excellence, holding spelling bees with the neighborhood children in our living room, and reading the classics aloud to Lori and me come evening. She welcomed all our friends from the neighborhood into our home, plying us with lemonade and tea sandwiches or her famous blueberry pancakes. She also encouraged us to be creative: she laughed delightedly when we drew pictures on our bedroom walls, and when our father complained, she said mildly, "Oh Lucien, they're just expressing themselves."

Daddy remained on the periphery of our lives, a remote figure who came and went on a schedule none of us could predict. I knew he had been married to another woman before he married our mother, whom he met at a dental convention in her hometown of Buffalo. After their nuptials, my mom had moved with Daddy to Joliet, where he already had an established dental practice, and where his first wife, Wilhelmina, and their two children also resided. Lori and I had met our older siblings, Bill and Linda, a few times, but for the most part, Daddy kept our two families apart. It was only after we all became independent adults that we were finally able to bond.

In time, Daddy began to stay away from the house on South Chicago Street more and more often. I confess, I was so used to his absences and his distant demeanor when he was around that I barely noticed at first. But then came an afternoon in my eleventh year, when Lori and I arrived home from school to find Mom at the kitchen table sobbing, a credit card statement spread flat on the table in front of her. Shaken by the sight of our mother so disarrayed, Lori went straight to her room. I approached her tentatively.

"Mommy, what's wrong?" I asked her, my heart hammering in my chest. The only other time I had ever seen her cry was when Dr. King was shot and killed. Every other day of my young life, Wilma Holman had been a strong, composed, and beautifully coiffed woman, her attractively rounded figure always impeccably attired. I thought my mother was the prettiest woman I knew, with her delicately pointed nose, full lips, and long oval face, just like mine. While Daddy was a firecracker, never one to hold back on expressing just what he thought, my mom was the quiet strength in our family. I was used to her managing our lives capably and decisively. She was our stalwart. I wanted to be just like her.

Now, she pulled me to her side and looked at me sadly. She ran a finger along my cheek and smoothed my hair.

"Your father and I are getting a divorce," she said, her voice thick with the effort to steady herself. "Your daddy is never coming back home."

I wish I could say I was surprised. It seemed to me that Daddy had been disappearing from our lives for ages. My more immediate concern was how Daddy's leaving would change things for our family. I hoped we would go on living in the house on South Chicago Street, and that life would continue much as before, but that was wishful thinking. Mom, Lori, and I would soon move from our solid redbrick house to a three-bedroom apartment on the west side of town, nearer to the recently integrated school Lori and I now attended.

Our family friends Tina Hernandez and her daughter Terry became our support system during those years, helping to care for Lori and me after Mom went back to nursing full time. Terry, two years my senior, was like a big sister. Her mother had once been a patient of my father's, before she became our live-in caretaker when Lori and I were very young. Tina and Wilma had grown as close as us three girls, and now Tina would once again look after our household while my mother worked.

Along with shifts at the hospital, Mom also enrolled in a master's program in nursing administration. She could usually be found studying at the kitchen table of our small apartment late into the night. Money was tight; I know that now, but my mother never blamed our father for our reduced circumstances. She wanted us to maintain a good relationship with him, and she took pains not to poison it. Even after she finished her master's program and moved our little family to Columbia, Maryland, in the summer before my senior year of high school, she did all she could to maintain an open channel to my father.

Daddy wasn't nearly as conscientious. Back when we still lived in Joliet, we seldom saw him after he moved out. Hungry for his notice, we looked forward to the two or three weekends each summer when he would invite us to sail Lake Michigan with him on his yacht.

One year, when Lori, Terry, and I arrived for our summer boat ride, Daddy introduced us to a walnut-brown woman in a broad-brimmed sun hat, and two brightly smiling little girls. Both girls wore pretty sundresses, and their hair was neatly done in two ribbon-tied braids. I was twelve that summer and Lori was eight. The little girls looked to be about five and three years old, and they stood serenely on the boat dock, next to my father. Daddy was holding a tiny hand of each girl, and they both leaned into him with an easy familiarity.

"That's Alma," Daddy told us, lifting his chin toward the woman in the sun hat. "And this is Danielle"—he raised the hand of the older girl—"and this is Alisa."

He spoke in an offhand way, not bothering to add: *these are your sisters*. But it was obvious at once. Little Alisa looked just like Daddy—the same round face, the same lemony skin and curly brown hair—and Danielle looked just like me. Alma was his third wife, and Danielle and Alisa were their daughters.

That afternoon on Lake Michigan, watching those sweet little girls clamber all over my father, observing his casual affection with them, I felt for the first time a crushing sense of loss. It seemed to me then that Daddy had well and truly left Lori and me, replacing us with these two beribboned girls on whom he showered more attention than he'd ever shown to us. It dawned on me that as remote as Daddy had always seemed when he lived with us, I had cast him as the hero of my childhood, the man who believed fervently in social justice, who championed the rights of our people, who put his shoe leather, and indeed his very life, on the line for his convictions.

That man now felt lost to me, my childhood in the civil rights movement almost a mirage, a dream that was fading to vapors. That day on the boat, when I met my beautiful little sisters for the first time, I felt as if I had been abandoned by my earliest and best example of living passionately for a purpose, of fighting tirelessly for a cause. Perhaps that is why the spirit of activism lay dormant in me for so many years, until another loss whipped it back to life.

CHAPTER 3

Stones from the River

IT WAS THE SUMMER OF 1988. I was in a good mood as I left the briefing room to walk to the plane with the rest of my in-flight crew. Wheeling my blue regulation carry-on bag behind me, I was looking forward to our overnight trip to New York. I'd be working first class with one of my favorite senior mamas—that's what we called those women who'd been on the job for going on twenty years, and who knew how to handle any situation on board. Reisha understood just when to cut off serving drinks to an intoxicated passenger, how to soothe a fearful traveler or crying child, and politely but firmly contain anyone who didn't accord her crew the proper respect. But these weren't the only reasons I was excited about working with Reisha. She had a wicked sense of humor and a generous heart, which would make the long hours pass quickly.

I was based in Dallas back then, having been assigned there five years before on completion of Delta's flight attendant training. "Hey, Luce," Reisha said as I stowed my overnight bag in the crew closet. "I hope you're ready for a full house. Everybody wants a taste of that New York life."

Across the country, the US presidential race was in full swing, with Ronald Reagan's vice president, George H. W. Bush, looking like the front-runner. The Republican campaign was already gearing up to deploy the "scary black man" tactic against Massachusetts governor Michael Dukakis, the leading Democratic contender. In the fall, the Republicans would air the devastating Willie Horton commercial, about an African American convict released on Massachusetts' weekend furlough program, only to rape a woman and stab her companion while he was out. The implication was clear: Dukakis would not protect voters from crime. Specifically, he would not protect them from *black* crime. For that, we needed to elect Bush Sr., the candidate who had taken out an NRA lifetime membership just prior to announcing his candidacy, the former CIA director who claimed to be against regulating firearms because "gun control does not work."[1]

Bush Sr. would famously resign from the NRA seven years later over what he termed their "rhetoric of hate," yet during his years in the Oval Office, his efforts to address gun safety legislation would be anemic at best. But none of this was on my mind that morning as I greeted the steady stream of first-class and Medallion Club passengers now boarding the plane. I completely failed to grasp the importance of electoral politics and the gun lobby to my future—and to the future of the man I would meet that very day.

In the galley, Reisha was arranging glasses on a silver tray covered with a starched white cloth, getting ready to offer water, juice, and champagne to our first-class travelers. When everyone was finally seated, their bags tucked away, and the first-class pre-takeoff drink service completed, I strolled through the cabin for a safety check, making sure seat belts had been fastened, seatbacks were in their upright position, and tray tables had been properly stowed. Then, as the plane pulled away from the gate and headed for the runway, I positioned myself at the front of the cabin to demonstrate in-flight emergency procedures.

As I pointed out the exits and explained the location of life vests, the operation of oxygen masks, and the use of flotation devices, I surveyed the cabin, trying to assess what kind of flight we would have that day. My eyes paused on the passenger in the left aisle seat, three rows back. I felt my heart quicken—good Lord, he was handsome. Lean and long-limbed in a crisp, blue button-down dress shirt and navy blue slacks with a razor crease, he had gleaming dark brown skin, a neat mustache, and closely cropped hair. At that moment he looked up, and his eyes locked onto mine with interest and amusement. He had sensed me noticing him. And now he was noticing me.

I smiled with embarrassment and looked away. This wasn't like me. I was warmly professional with passengers, just as I'd been trained to be. I certainly wasn't in the habit of exchanging coy glances while showing them how to blow into the red tubes that inflate the life vest in the event of a water landing.

After finishing up the safety demonstration, I retreated to the galley and buckled myself into the jump seat for takeoff. I reached for the clipboard that held the manifest, wanting to check the name of the passenger in Seat 3C.

I looked at Reisha, who was strapped into the jump seat across from me. "Do you know the man in 3C?" I asked her. "It says he works for Delta."

Reisha winked at me. "That one's a charmer," she said. "You be careful, Luce."

She told me that Mr. 3C was in reservation sales. Around the time that I started with the airline, he had moved from his native New York to become a gate agent in Jacksonville, Florida. He often non-revved back to New York to see his family in Queens, connecting through Dallas, which was how she'd gotten to know him.

Later, as I maneuvered the beverage cart down the aisle during meal service, I could feel the gate agent's eyes on me. He flirted openly whenever I handed him something—water, tomato juice, his meal, coffee, a glass of wine. I suspected he kept dreaming up new requests just so I'd keep coming by his seat. He asked me where I was from, and told me my smile was beautiful. He wanted to know when he could see me again. I felt as giddy as a schoolgirl with a crush, unable to stop beaming. I was so flustered by his attention that I busied myself in the galley as much as I could so as to stay out of the cabin. I was sure everyone could see the effect that the tall, athletically built man in Seat 3C was having on me. The chemistry between us was so palpable that the passenger seated next to him teased, "Hey, man, I don't think I'm getting the same level of service that you are."

Ronald Davis exuded charisma. By the time he told me he had been raised in South Ozone Park, Queens, and that he hoped I'd let him show me the city from the perspective of a New Yorker, I was smitten.

"Maybe next time we're both in New York," I said casually, not wanting to seem overly eager. But I already knew I wanted to see him again, and so when, at the end of the flight, he waited till all the other passengers had disembarked, and then walked up and asked me for my number, I gave it willingly.

We chatted a bit more as he strolled with me to the shuttle bus that was waiting outside to take the crew to our hotel. As we said our goodbyes at the curb, I remember thinking there was a good chance I might never hear from him again. Yet he called me the very next day to ask when my schedule would take me back to New York. He planned to meet me there and make good on his offer. Although my itinerary often had me doing layovers in New York, I knew very little about the city. It seemed like a vast, cosmopolitan metropolis, mysterious to me, and so I happily agreed to let Ron show me the town.

For the next few months, almost every time I flew to New York on an overnight, Ron would arrange to be there. I soon learned he had been married before, and had a nine-year-old son who lived in Queens with his ex-wife. While Ron was eager for me to know his firstborn, I was nervous that the child would resent me out of loyalty to his mother, much as I had resented my father's third wife when I first met her that day on the boat ride. I need not have worried. Ronnie was a shy and sweet-natured boy, and we hit it off at once. In years to come, we would forge a warm, affectionate relationship that endures to this day.

That summer, Ron took me all over the city, showing me the sights. We held hands while exploring Central Park and saw Nancy Wilson perform at the Blue Note. We climbed to the top of the Empire State Building, viewed the Statue of Liberty from the deck of the Staten Island Ferry, and wandered through recreated pyramids inside the Metropolitan Museum of Art. As summer turned to fall and then to winter, I realized I was falling in love.

Ron and I began to spend time together back home, non-revving between Jacksonville and Dallas whenever we had days off. We met each other's friends, but mostly, we stayed in our own enchanted bubble. Then, on a weekend in July, almost one year to the day after we met, Ron booked us on a harbor cruise in Jacksonville. We sailed out to a white sand beach where we swam and picnicked and got to know our fellow day-trippers. On the way back across the harbor late that afternoon, Ron suddenly got down on one knee in front of me. He reached into his pocket and brought out a hinged blue velvet box. He snapped it open to reveal a gold ring.

"Lucy, marry me!" he said, more a command than a question. But then his confidence was part of what had attracted me.

Not having suspected that we were anywhere close to this point in our relationship, I was shocked, although I confess I had often thought, *I could marry this man.* At twenty-eight years old, footloose and traveling the world, I was in no rush to walk down the aisle. Yet, suddenly, the decision was upon me, and with the whole cruise looking on, and the setting sun bleeding pink and orange overhead, I laughed and pulled him to his feet and said, "Yes, Ron. I will marry you."

We exchanged our vows at the botanical gardens in Dallas the following October. As breathtaking as the setting was, holding the ceremony outdoors was a mistake. It was a blazing hot day, the humidity pressing down on us like a moist blanket, and on top of that, my mother was showing the first signs of dementia: she couldn't remember the names of people she'd known for years, and she seemed generally disoriented and confused. My father didn't make it to my wedding at all. He had been diagnosed with blood clots in his legs, and his doctor forbade him to fly to Dallas from Chicago. Just one month later, a clot would break free and become lodged in his heart, causing catastrophic heart failure. My father, whom I had yearned to know more fully for my entire life, left us for good just before Thanksgiving 1989.

———

I didn't move in with my new husband right away. Compared to Dallas, Jacksonville felt small and provincial to me. People were friendly enough, but most of the relationships I'd formed there tended to be superficial, like a smile that didn't make it all the way to the eyes. Besides, my job was based in Dallas. To live with Ron full time, I'd have to transfer my airport hub to Atlanta, which was only thirty minutes by air from Jacksonville, compared to my usual three-hour flight from Dallas. Still, I resisted making the change.

For six months, Ron tolerated my reluctance to leave my condo and my thriving social life in Dallas. Our long-distance arrangement was only feasible because our non-rev benefits allowed us to fly back and forth to see each other every weekend. But then Eastern, one of our standby airlines, shut down its Jacksonville route, reducing our non-rev options. That's when I finally decided to move my base of operations to Atlanta and commute to work from Jacksonville. Ron was happy to finally have his wife sharing his home, but the constant travel back and forth to Atlanta for flight assignments was wearying, especially since I didn't have a condo there as I'd had in Dallas. I was spending more time in airports waiting for my shift to start than in my own bed. After a year of this, I convinced Ron that we needed to move to Atlanta, where there were better professional growth opportunities for us both.

In the summer of 1990, Ron rented out his condo in Jacksonville and we moved to an apartment in the Atlanta suburb of College Park. We bought a plot of land in Villa Rica, about an hour west of the city, and began drawing up plans to build a two-story contemporary home nestled in a cul-de-sac surrounded by scenic woods. At last I felt sufficiently settled in my living situation and my work schedule that I could think about starting our family.

But this would not prove simple for us. In fact, trying to have a baby would turn out to be one of the most difficult trials of our marriage. After two miscarriages, I began to despair of ever carrying to term. I finally got pregnant again, and all seemed to be going well. I learned that I was carrying a boy, and I decided to name him Lucien, after my father. I imagined my dad in heaven would look down and smile at my naming choice, and now, with full understanding of how I had yearned to be closer to him, he would wrap his daughter and his namesake in his protection and care. Perhaps that was hubris on my part, an effort to bargain with God. It didn't work. At four months, I began to bleed profusely. I rushed to the emergency room, where my doctor broke the news that I had suffered a fetal demise due to the overgrowth of a large fibroid on the back wall of my uterus. I had to be admitted to the hospital to deliver Lucien naturally. That night was excruciating—the pain of labor and no hope of a living child.

Family and friends tried to comfort me. "You're young, you can try again," they'd say, but their well-meaning words haunted me. I wanted nothing more passionately than I wanted to birth and raise my own child, but what if God had decided I was not worthy of becoming a mother? How would I make peace with that?

I was on the verge of giving up hope, when my doctor suggested I have a myomectomy to remove my fibroids. A year after the surgery, I got pregnant again. This time, my doctor was taking no chances. She put me on bed rest almost from the beginning. Concerned that my womb, now half its pre-surgery size, might restrict my baby's growth, she monitored me closely. She needn't have worried. This baby was active. I sat on my couch for nine long months feeling him kick vigorously. He was making space for himself inside there. I couldn't wait to meet him.

My doctor scheduled a C-section two weeks before my due date. My baby boy arrived at 7:16 AM on February 16, 1995. He weighed 7 pounds, 6½ ounces, and was 21½ inches tall. These details matter more than ever to me now. Just like the tiny inked footprint that we carried with us from the hospital on the day we took our newborn home, these concrete facts are proof that my beautiful child was here, on this earth with me, for seventeen years.

Ron and I had agreed that if I gave birth to a girl, he would choose the name, and if we had a boy, I would be the one to name him. Secretly, I had known all along that I was having a boy. I had lost so many pregnancies that I didn't want my doctor to withhold a single detail about this one. Every new piece of information brought with it the assurance that my baby was gestating exactly as he should. But I didn't tell Ron that I knew the gender. He had said that he wanted to be surprised.

During those long homebound months that I sat waiting for our son's arrival, I began to read the Bible more closely than I ever had before. I would read and pray over my growing child, asking God to care for him, and to raise him up in abiding faith. By the time I finally held my squalling newborn in my arms, I had already decided to name him in homage to the biblical story of God holding back the floodwaters of the river Jordan, allowing the ancient Hebrews to cross into Canaan, out of reach of their enemies. My favorite detail of this story, recounted in the Book of Joshua, chapters three and four, was when the Lord had instructed the leader of the Israelites to have his priests retrieve twelve stones from the riverbed as a reminder of how their Heavenly Father had delivered his faithful across the rushing water to the Promised Land. Once safely in Canaan, Joshua had stacked the stones to create a memorial, a reminder that God would always guide and protect his children. In naming my only son Jordan, I was bestowing upon him the promise of those stones from the river—asking God to love and protect my child, and deliver him to his life's great purpose, his own Promised Land. How was I to guess what God would one day ask of us in fulfillment of that very prayer?

I have no doubt that my child knew he was born to do God's work. Later, when he was at his most rambunctious stage, and I was upset at him about something, he'd say to me, "Don't be mad, Mommy. Remember, you prayed for me. You prayed for me to come to you. You watch and see. I'm going to do something special. I know, because you prayed for me to be here." My son reminded me of this often when he was growing up. And it calmed me every time. "Okay, Jordan," I'd say. "I don't doubt you. But you still have to clean up your room." I think deep down in his spirit Jordan always knew that God had a special assignment for him. And from the moment I heard his first cry I believed it, too. But it would be years before I grasped an even greater truth—that, whether or not we choose to accept it, God holds special assignments for us all.

CHAPTER 4

Caregiver

THAT FIRST YEAR WITH JORDAN was everything I had imagined family life could be. Ron adored his son, and was a romantic partner to me. I was living the fantasy I had yearned for in my childhood, especially after my father left our home. We even managed to get away on a vacation to Guadalajara for a week, with Ron's sainted mother, we called her Mama Davis, moving into our home to take care of Jordan while we were gone. After barely smiling for his first six months, which had worried me, Jordan blossomed into a gregarious and curious toddler. At ten months, he just got up and started walking one day, laughing from the depths of his little body. Ron and I were completely in love—with each other and with our beautiful boy. I was so wrapped up in the idyll of our little family I didn't notice the dark clouds gathering.

Some years before Jordan was born, I had visited my mom in Columbia, Maryland. She still lived in the same house we had moved to from Joliet in the summer before my senior year of high school. We'd lived with my aunt Arlene, who had been lonely and depressed, and welcomed having her sister and her two nieces sharing the house.

On my last visit, I couldn't help noticing that the disorientation Mom had exhibited at my wedding had deepened. Later, we would suspect that her apparent dementia had been complicated by a series of small, undiagnosed strokes.

I made the hard decision to move Mom to Atlanta to live with me. I was newly pregnant with Lucien then, and had reduced my flying schedule to just the weekends so as not to stress the pregnancy. I figured I'd be able to take care of Mom during the week, and Ron could pitch in when I had to fly.

"How on earth can you care for your mother with a new baby on the way?" Ron argued when I called to tell him Mom would be returning home with me. "Maybe you should hire a home aide to take care of her where she is."

There was no way. This was my mother we were talking about. She had sacrificed so much for Lori and me. But when, just a couple of months into her living with us, I lost baby Lucien, I had to admit I needed help. Mom required more consistent daily care than I was truly able to give her. My relief at having my mother so close to me was edged by distress at Wilma's own frustration at no longer being independent—she hated having to rely on others, and I was so tapped out with doing, doing, doing that I could barely take care of myself. At night I would fall into bed beside Ron exhausted. I was so sleep-deprived I thought sometimes I was going insane.

Then, in February 1994, Mom suffered a major stroke. As part of her recovery, she moved into Emory Hospital's Stroke Center for two months, and then into a senior apartment at an assisted living facility located near to the house we were building in Villa Rica. She took her meals with other residents in a communal dining room there, and skilled caregivers checked in on her daily, helping to bathe and groom her, and performing light housekeeping tasks like laundry. I visited every day, overseeing her adjustment, but that meant spending long hours away from home.

Life got a bit easier when our house in Villa Rica was completed and we finally moved in. We were now only minutes away from my mother's senior living apartment. But after I got pregnant with Jordan and my doctor put me on bed rest, I could no longer drive to visit my mother, so Ron brought her to me. Mom seemed supremely at peace as she sat on our large back deck gazing out at the woods, or wandering through the rooms of our airy, light-filled home. After Jordan was born, she loved nothing more than to sit holding him beside a window overlooking our garden, but this respite didn't last. Just before Jordan's first birthday, Mom suffered a second stroke, which left her more debilitated than before. We had no choice but to move her to a facility where she could receive more intensive nursing care. The best one was almost an hour away, and so I was back to commuting long distances to see her—except now, I also had Jordan.

Ron suggested we hire a babysitter, and we did. She helped out a lot with Jordan but the care of my steadily declining mother still fell to me.

"You spend so much time with your mother you aren't even thinking about me," Ron grumbled one night when I arrived home after eleven. It was now the fall of 1996, Jordan was almost two years old, and Mom had recently suffered a third stroke. It had left her blind in one eye, paralyzed on one side, and completely bedridden. I had decided to move her to a nursing home nearer our house, so I could get to her more easily. That evening, she'd been having a particularly hard time getting settled. She didn't recognize any of the nurses at the new place, even though they had been caring for her for almost a month by then. I remained her one anchor to the world, and I had been loath to leave her. I recalled the capable and fun-loving woman who'd engineered such good times for Lori and me while we were growing up. I looked past the fear and uncertainty swimming in the depths of her one good eye, and saw the single mother who had folded away her own heartbreak so as to create a comfortable middle-class existence for her daughters. I saw the nurse who had gone back to graduate school so as to better provide for her family, the bold woman who had moved us across the country to start a new life in Maryland. I wanted so much to protect her now, to take away her confusion, to give her back the self she knew. But all I could do that night was sit at her bedside, stroking the tangle of veins on her wrinkled hand and smoothing the damp hair from her forehead.

All this weighed on my heart as I walked into the house. I wanted only to make my way to Jordan's room, to stand over his crib, place my hand lightly on his back, and comfort myself with the rise and fall of his breathing as he slept. Instead, Ron met me in the kitchen, annoyed at the lateness of my arrival. "I had to eat dinner alone and put Jordan to bed myself—again," he complained.

"Ron," I said, my voice weary. "You're grown. You can manage. I need to be there for my mom. You know that."

That was probably the night I realized we were in trouble, and that a distance had crept into our marriage. Perhaps I hadn't noticed it happening because the reserve between Ron and me was so much more polite than the open antagonism I remembered between my parents when they were breaking up. It was true that Ron and I didn't communicate much these days, except to coordinate our schedules as they affected Jordan. And I was so busy with my caregiving duties we hadn't had a date night in months. But surely this distance was only temporary. I knew my mother would not be with us much longer. I couldn't fathom my world without her, and it was only the thought of being with Ron and Jordan that helped me bear her last days.

After Wilma stopped breathing on Christmas Eve 1996, I could barely get out of bed. I took time off from work, and released our babysitter, wanting to close ranks as I mourned. I hoped that once it was just the three of us again, we'd be able to recapture some of the magic and connection of Jordan's first year. But instead of getting better, things got worse. I couldn't seem to muster enthusiasm for anything or anyone but my baby boy. All I wanted was to sit and stare, rousing myself only to take care of Jordan. What had been a crack in Ron and my relationship now became a chasm. I knew we needed to find our way back to each other, and that I couldn't navigate the path alone. I argued that we needed the help of a couples' therapist, and grudgingly, Ron agreed to go.

In our sessions, Ron was mostly glowering and uncooperative until, at our third meeting, the therapist called him on his attitude. "Do you really want this marriage?" she asked him. "Because you're not acting as if you're even willing to try."

Ron stood up abruptly, his tall, athletic frame filling the small room.

"You're right," he said. "I don't want to do this anymore. I think we need to separate."

I sat in stunned silence as he stalked out of the room.

"You know, Luce," he told me that evening, "the first six years of our marriage were great. But once you started taking care of your mother, it went downhill fast."

I could hardly believe what he was telling me. It was several moments before I found my voice. "Ron," I said finally, my tone deceptively calm, "I hope and pray your mother never gets sick like mine did. I hope that you never have to give as much of your life to caring for your parent as I had to. But if it should ever come to that, I know you will be man enough to do what I did for my mother. She *needed* me. Did you actually think I would walk away from her? I hope you're not blaming this on my mother."

"I'm your husband," Ron said. "I needed your time and attention, too—"

I didn't wait to hear any more. I went to find Jordan. He was playing with a stuffed tiger in his room. His little arms reached for me as I stooped to pick him up. I cradled him against my shoulder, my heart sore. I now knew that he would not get to grow up in a house with both his parents. I didn't fear that Ron would abandon him; he loved him so much, and was a good father. But for Jordan, being with one of his parents would now forever mean that he would be missing the other. It felt like a generational curse, the ache of my youth now visited on my son.

I nuzzled his neck and hoped that I would do as well for him as my mother had done for Lori and me. I held his wriggling body closer and breathed in the little boy scent of him. "Please, God," I whispered. "Please." I didn't even know what I was asking for in that burdened prayer. Jordan was not yet three.

———

I was supposed to leave for a three-day trip the next morning, but I was a basket case, my spirit absolutely crushed, so I called in sick to my supervisor. I didn't tell Ron that I wouldn't be flying after all— I needed time to think, to compose myself, to figure out what came next. Instead, I called one of my friends, a fellow flight attendant. She was scheduled to fly, too, but she offered me the downstairs apartment in her home as a refuge while she was gone. I stayed there alone for three days, on my knees, sobbing and pouring my heart out to God.

"Lord," I cried. "Why is this happening to us?"

I begged him to take away my pain. I knew I could not be who I needed to be for Jordan if I held on to the corrosive bitterness I was feeling toward his father. I also knew I had to be strategic: if my marriage was indeed over, I needed to make sure that Jordan and I could flourish and have a good life on our own. Ron and I would have to negotiate in good faith what was best for our child, but on one detail I would not be moved: Jordan was staying with me. And so, as the tears rolled down my face, I prayed to be delivered from my sense of betrayal, regret, anger, and sorrow. I prayed for strength and clarity. I prayed for wisdom and divine guidance. I prayed for Jordan.

On the third night, an unexpected peace descended over me. My tears dried. I became perfectly still. And in the quiet of my thoughts, I discerned the voice of God speaking directly to me for the first time in my life: *Your work is finished here. You must move on. I will bring you a village to protect the child.*

CHAPTER 5

Paper Boat

JORDAN WAS AT THE FAR end of the gray hallway, slumped in a desk-and-chair combo that was too small for his long, skinny, six-year-old frame. His elbows were propped on the desk, his chin resting on his palms, his fingers fanned like angel wings against his cheeks. My chest tightened. Jordan's teacher had put him out of his first-grade classroom again, which meant she believed his behavior that afternoon left something to be desired.

This had been happening with distressing regularity. Even more upsetting, I never saw any child but Jordan, and occasionally the other black boy in his group, let's call him Brandon, banished from the classroom. Never did I arrive to pick my son up from school and see a white child sitting in the hall. Yet on at least two occasions each week, I'd find my son or Brandon in the hallway whiling away the minutes till class ended. And even on those afternoons when I picked Jordan up from inside the classroom, too often I'd note that his little paper boat on the behavior chart had sunk to the bottom of the blue construction-paper ocean.

I couldn't understand it: Why would a teacher at a Christian private school a mere thirty minutes outside of Atlanta, the so-called Black Mecca of the South, consistently send *only* the two black boys to the hallway? Surely Jordan and Brandon, in a class of twenty children, weren't the only ones who ever acted up? Didn't any of the white children ever need to be disciplined? Apparently not, because week after week the story never changed—and it was taking its toll on my son. I could see my bright, curious, energetic child literally folding in on himself, shutting down his eagerness for the world, bewildered and hurt to the core.

"Why is Jordan in the hallway?" I'd ask his teacher.

She was in her late twenties and had a master's in early childhood education, even though she looked not much older than a teenager. She wore her hair pulled back in a blond ponytail, and she was unfailingly peppy with the mothers who served as classroom helpers. When I inquired about Jordan being sent out of class yet again, she would earnestly explain that she just didn't know what to do with my son. "He blurts out the answers to questions without raising his hand, and he's always talking to his friends," she would tell me.

"But if he's talking to his friends, then they are talking to him, too," I'd point out, "yet he's the only one who gets put outside."

"No, no, it's not like that," she'd assure me. "Most of the other kids settle down after a while."

At home, when I asked Jordan for his side of the story, he would invariably tell me something like this: "Well, Mark and Brandon and Joey and me were talking about Power Rangers, and then they sent Brandon and me to the hallway." Jordan would scrunch up his little face and peer at me. "I don't think it's fair that only Brandon and me got in trouble. We weren't being bad."

"You're right, Jordan," I'd say. "You weren't being bad. You're a good kid, and I want you to understand that I know that."

I would then explain to Jordan how important it was for him to listen to his teacher, and to behave himself in class. That meant being attentive during the lessons and not talking and laughing with his friends when the teacher wanted the kids to be quiet. And no matter how eager he was to show he knew the response to a question, he should wait to be called on rather than just shout the answer out. Let the teacher teach, I told him.

Jordan tried to contain himself. I know he did. But he was a naturally exuberant child, and learning new things excited him. He was also incredibly sweet natured, so I couldn't fathom why his teacher hadn't found a way to work with him. When Jordan started asking me, "Mom, why am I always the bad kid?" I knew I had to take the next step. No matter how often I told my son that he was as good and kind and smart as every other child in the class, he was beginning to think of himself as a troublemaker. My happy and compliant little boy had grown tense and quiet in the mornings before school. He recognized the unfairness of what was happening more clearly than he could express, and it just didn't sit right with him that he so often got punished for things the other kids also did.

I decided to spend some time as a classroom mom so I could observe the situation for myself. It was during those weeks as a parent volunteer that I really became convinced the teacher had targeted my child—and I was part of the reason.

I quickly noticed that all the storybooks included in the first-grade curriculum, and all the assigned projects, featured families in which there was a mommy and a daddy living together in a child's home. Nowhere was a family like ours visible. It didn't help that Jordan was the only child in his classroom whose parents were divorced. Now I began to understand his searching questions about his father: "Why doesn't my daddy live with us? Artis's and Brandon's fathers live with them. Why isn't my daddy at home with me?" I would hasten to comfort him that he had done nothing wrong to make his father move out, and that both his parents loved him deeply. But my urgent assurances barely concealed the painful truth I knew—that when my own father left home, no explanation ever lessened my sense of abandonment.

Now, belatedly, I realized that there was another dimension to Jordan being the only child of divorced parents in his group, one that I had naively overlooked: in that predominantly white evangelical Christian school, I was the stereotypical embodiment of a black single mother raising an unruly black boy alone. Jordan's teacher appeared to be acting on beliefs she'd unconsciously absorbed from media and pop culture portrayals of families like ours. It was a soup in which she had been marinating all her life, along with every other person born and raised in this country. The cop shows she flipped past with the television remote, the news stories of crime in urban neighborhoods, the books she'd read, movies she'd watched, comments tossed off by family and friends—all of it added up to deep-seated assumptions about my son and me that I hadn't even known I needed to address.

Unfortunately, the sort of implicit bias Jordan and I were now facing is harder to root out than overt prejudice. As Harvard sociologist Dr. David Williams points out, when people discriminate based on subconscious ideas about a group, they don't even realize they're doing it. "The research shows that when bias is unconscious it is also automatic," Williams says, adding that 70 to 80 percent of Americans operate based on subliminal racial cues. "This discriminatory behavior is activated more quickly and effortlessly than conscious discrimination, more quickly than saying, 'I've decided to discriminate against this person.'"[1]

Williams observes that implicit bias represents an evolution in the way racism is understood and expressed in American life. "Sixty years ago, most people in America believed that blacks were biologically inferior, inherently inferior, they were made by God inferior," he explains. "Today there is a cultural racism that says black parents are not giving their children the right values, and it's often offered as a reason for why blacks are not doing as well as other groups or as well as they could. It associates *black* with a range of negative characteristics that are so deeply embedded in American culture that people who hold these ideas are not bad people. They're just good Americans. Because it's what American society has taught them."[2]

Williams and a team of social scientists compiled a database of ten million words from books, newspapers, magazine articles, and documents, all representing what average college-educated Americans are exposed to over the course of their lifetimes. "When the word *black* occurs in American culture," Williams says, "what tends to co-occur is *poor* and *violent* and *religious* but also *lazy*, *cheerful*, *dangerous*. Being *violent*, *lazy* and *dangerous*, other contemporary public opinion research shows, are negative stereotypes of blacks widely endorsed by the American public. All racial ethnic minority groups are stereotyped more negatively than whites, with blacks viewed the worst, then Latinos, who are viewed twice as negatively as Asians."[3]

But how would I help Jordan's teacher see that certain attitudes, of which she might not even be aware, could be shaping her behavior toward my son and Brandon? It was a long-standing story, documented by educational researchers in one study after another: black boys are labeled as "disruptive," while white boys who exhibit the same behaviors are labeled as merely "active." In September 2016, for example, the Yale Child Study Center found that elementary school teachers, both black and white, monitor the behavior of black boys in their classroom much more closely than that of other children. In the study, 135 teachers were shown videos of four elementary-school children playing and interacting in a room. The children were a black boy, a white boy, a black girl, and a white girl. The teachers were asked to identify and rate any challenging behavior they observed on the part of the children. The rub? None of the children in the video exhibited any challenging behavior, yet 42 percent of the teachers identified the black boy's behavior as problematic. Eye-tracking technology also revealed that all the teachers spent more time watching the black children, especially the black boy.[4] "Implicit biases do not begin with black men and police," the study's lead researcher, Walter Gilliam, notes. "They begin with young black boys and their preschool teachers, if not earlier."[5]

I became more fully aware of these kinds of academic studies long after Jordan had moved on from first grade, but I didn't need to have read them to know that what he was experiencing in the classroom was not my imagination. From the beginning, I'd noticed that Jordan's teacher was markedly more formal with me than with any of the white mothers who volunteered in her classroom, or who came to collect their children at the end of the day. I observed the easy warmth with which she greeted those other mothers, and compared it to her wary coolness with me. It perplexed me at first, because I was used to navigating integrated environments, and I got along with people from various backgrounds. As Jordan's mother, I had expected that his teacher and I would team up to ensure Jordan's success. Instead, I now felt duty bound to point out that she was exhibiting bias toward my son.

I should not have been surprised that she became defensive. "We do not discriminate at this school, Mrs. Davis," she said, her arms folded stiffly across her chest. "We are not racist here."

No doubt Jordan's teacher truly believed that she did not treat my son any differently from the other children. At the level of consciousness, she sincerely assumed herself to be unbiased, insisting that she was simply responding to Jordan's behavior in the moment.

"There's often an undercurrent of fear or tension between black male students and many white teachers, and even some black ones," says Harry Morgan, an early childhood development professor at the State University of West Georgia, who has studied classroom interaction between teachers and students for more than thirty years. "This fear can be triggered over something as minor as a black boy walking around the room. On some subliminal level, the teacher is afraid to have even a very young black male defy the simplest rule. She's afraid his defiance will escalate."[6]

Whether or not Jordan's teacher was aware of the underlying beliefs that shaped her everyday behavior, once I witnessed it for myself, I could not continue to allow my son to be subject to such bias. I decided to take my concerns to the school's principal, but that would turn out to be equally unsatisfying. The principal suggested I get Jordan tested for ADHD, which I did, only to have the tester confirm what I already knew—that Jordan was an intelligent, inquisitive, energetic child who had all the tools to thrive in a mainstream classroom, if positively engaged. The principal didn't seem to know what to do with the tester's report. She offered mildly that she would speak to Jordan's teacher.

It was almost the end of the school year by then, and in fact Jordan never again got put out of his first-grade classroom, although Brandon continued to be sent to the hallway on occasion, possibly because his parents chose not to address the issue with the school. I prayed for months about the situation, and the answer that came was that I needed to extricate my child from an environment in which he and boys who looked like him were not prized. In a Christian school, this state of affairs was especially disheartening, because hadn't Jesus asked us, above all, to love our neighbors?

CHAPTER 6

Finding Faith

IN ONE SENSE, I BLAMED myself for the trouble Jordan was having with his first-grade teacher. I hadn't sufficiently investigated the public school district in which I had chosen to raise my son. He was only three when we moved to Douglasville; I was still grieving the breakdown of my marriage, and the last thing on my mind was where Jordan would attend school. By the time I realized my mistake—that I had bought a home in a district where many of the public schools earned a failing grade—Jordan was ready to start pre-kindergarten. I decided to enroll him in a nearby Christian private school that one of my neighbors recommended, because more than anything I wanted my son to grow up knowing and loving God.

I also wanted to raise my son in a safe, middle-class community, in a beautifully appointed home that would shield us from the stigma of my single motherhood, which I confess I was already feeling. And so, as soon as Ron moved out of the home we'd built together in Villa Rica, I put the house on the market. The rooms I had hoped to fill with children were now cavernous and empty with just Jordan and me. I awoke on June 1, 1999, feeling particularly forlorn. It was my thirty-ninth birthday. Ron had been gone for three months, and there was a tremendous void where our dreams once breathed, an oppressive absence that stilled the air. Impulsively, I woke Jordan up and told him that we were going to the county animal shelter that very morning to get a dog.

I can still see the two of us, walking up and down the shelter aisle, looking for just the right animal. And there, at the back of one cage sat a very quiet but obviously well cared for Pointer mixed breed. The dog's previous owners had named him Freckles, because of the white spots that dotted his sand-colored coat. As he gazed at us with calm, expectant eyes, I knew he was exactly the addition to our household that we needed, the perfect canine companion for Jordan. Oh, how my son loved that dog. They followed each other everywhere. Seeing my son so happy with Freckles eased my sore heart a bit.

By October, I had sold our home and moved with my three-year-old into a one-bedroom model apartment in Douglasville, about forty-five minutes southwest of Atlanta. I was determined that our stay in the model apartment would be temporary, especially now that we had a dog. Three months later, I found what I thought was the perfect house in a well-kept and racially integrated neighborhood. The house was a stately white three-story colonial with black wood shutters, tucked at the end of a cul-de-sac. Dogwoods, crepe myrtles, Bradford pears, and oak trees shaded the large lot, and at the back of the house, two decks opened onto a spacious yard. A door inside the two-car garage led into a gleaming white kitchen with pristine hardwood floors. In years to come, Jordan and I would spend many hours conversing at the counter in that kitchen. He would ask me probing questions while I cooked his favorite meals, and as he grew older, he would bring friends to commune at our table and seek my counsel, too.

Upstairs, large dormer windows overlooked the front of the house, allowing me to keep track of Jordan and his friends from the neighborhood as they played in the cul-de-sac. I could hear Jordan issuing directions to the other boys, always the leader of their games. A wooded lot sat adjacent to us, and in the fall, Jordan would gather the boys to rake up the mountains of leaves that blew into our yard. I can still see the boys out there, rakes in their hands, laughing over their labor, just as I can still see Jordan and Freckles in the den of that house, napping under tents that my son had built using blankets and chairs. Apart from the unfortunate situation playing out at school, our life on that street was charmed.

When I bought the house, I thought I had calculated all the variables: How long would it take me to get to work; was the neighborhood friendly; were there kids on the block for Jordan to play with; was there a Christian congregation nearby that I could join? I had even asked some of the neighbors about the schools in our district, and they'd assured me they were fine. In fact, many of these same parents had sent their children to private institutions, and weren't really in a position to assess the public schools. My mistake was that I didn't do my own research, which is how Jordan ended up at the Christian academy.

Some good did come out of Jordan starting out in that school: I found my way back to the church through some of our fellow African American families. Bishop Artis Crum and his wife, Cassandra, had a son in the same grade as Jordan, though not in the same classroom. Whatever they might have heard about Jordan and me, the Crums immediately embraced us. They offered us support at a crucial time. Artis Jr. and Jordan had become buddies in kindergarten, which had led to their parents also becoming close. On weekends when I had to fly for Delta, it was the Crums who looked after Jordan, except on those occasions when he spent the weekend with his father in Jacksonville. The Crums folded Jordan in with their own children, enrolling him in Sunday school at Light and Salvation Outreach, the evangelical church

Artis Sr. pastored. My weekend schedule chafed sometimes, but it also allowed me to be a room mom at school, to chaperone field trips, and to make sure Jordan got to after-school baseball practice on time. When Cassandra invited Jordan and me to join them for Wednesday evening Bible study, I was thrilled to discover an alternative to Sunday worship. Walking through the doors of that sanctuary for the first time, I felt as if I had at last returned to my Christian faith, which I had practiced somewhat intermittently in the years before Jordan was born.

As much as Artis and Cassandra welcomed me into their small, intimate church, however, and as much as they supported and loved Jordan, something was still missing in my spiritual life. I felt so ready to explore and deepen my faith, and I thought the best way to do that would be through deeds—to do the work of the church in every way possible. I wanted to grow, I wanted to serve, I wanted to learn, but the church leaders didn't seem inclined to put any responsibility in my hands. They would dole out committee memberships, stewardship roles, and lay ministry positions to other members of the congregation, always overlooking my requests to get involved.

A little voice inside me whispered that it was because I was divorced. I suspected that even though people were kind and warm to me, the church leaders held my single mother status against me, as if I were somehow tainted because I had failed to uphold the sanctity of my marriage, tearing asunder what God had joined together. I tried to rationalize it away: I was a working mom, too busy to truly commit; I was newly returned to the church, a brand-new Christian in their eyes. These were perfectly reasonable arguments. Indeed, I repeated them to myself again and again. And yet, in my quest to learn all I could by serving God actively, not passively, I felt squelched. I didn't yet understand that worshipful prayer can be one of the most dynamic ways to serve. I never complained as the church leaders passed me over again and again, but inwardly, I was as hurt and confused as Jordan in his first-grade classroom. The truth was, since my divorce, I'd felt like a perpetual outsider, not just at the Christian private school, but also in the church community I had chosen for our little family. Spiritually and emotionally, I was floundering.

At a school event one evening, I shared my frustrations with two of my other African American parent friends, Conrad and Yvette Maynard. Jordan was in second grade by then, and I'd had high hopes for an improvement over his first-grade experience, particularly because his teacher that year was a black woman. I'd felt sure she would *see* my child, value his eagerness to please, and engage his excitement about learning. But the start of the year had not gone well: Jordan, it turned out, had already been labeled as disruptive, and that reputation followed him into the new academic year. One morning, while serving as a mother helper, I watched as Jordan skipped across the classroom to place a couple of errant blocks in their proper bin. Jarringly, his teacher yelled at him to take his place on the circle mat where the other children were gathering in preparation for reading. Her tone was angry and scolding. Jordan did as he was told, but the hurt and bewilderment on his face pierced me.

I had already decided to remove my son from that school, but I didn't yet know how I would manage my weekend flying schedule without the help of the Crums and other families like the Maynards and the McKays, who had been so supportive of Jordan and me. The fact that our boys attended the same academy had made our arrangements seamless, but how would it work when I transferred Jordan to another school? I also hated the idea of separating my son from his best friend, Artis Jr., especially since I was already contemplating finding a new spiritual home.

Yvette Maynard didn't see this as an insurmountable problem.

"Oh, Jordan and Artis and the other boys can still get together out-side of school," she told me. "But if you're not feeling fulfilled in your spiritual life, Lucy, well, nothing else is going to feel quite right."

And then Yvette extended the invitation that would transform my relationship with God: "Why don't you come visit our church and see how you like it?"

"I can promise you won't feel like an outsider there," Conrad chimed in. "We have all kinds of families, including several headed by single moms. Maybe you could start a single parent ministry."

"I'll tell you what," Yvette said, "the next Sunday you have off, we'll pick you and Jordan up for services. Oh, honey, you're going to love our church."

———

Trinity Chapel Church of God felt like coming home. I fell in love with the diversity of the congregation. It was deeply healing to be around people of so many different colors and ethnicities, and families of all descriptions. I treasured the way everyone joined together to worship God, enjoying rather than ignoring one another's differences. To me, Trinity Chapel looked like the America my parents had imag-ined and fought for back in the sixties.

Over the next decade, my roots would grow deep in that church, and my faith would multiply by leaps and bounds. I did indeed find a single parent ministry there, along with two other black single moms, a white single mom, and a black single dad. We offered one another spiritual support in whatever ways might be needed.

For Jordan and me, with no extended family in or around Atlanta, the congregation at Trinity became our kin. Best of all, they recognized my son's goodness, which, after his experience at the Christian academy, was a balm to me. "We love Jordan," they told me. "He is such a sweet kid, such a loving kid, such a funny kid, and that is a testament to how you're raising him." They *believed* in my child. They saw his true nature. They looked beyond the fact that my son and I fit an American stereotype that was so often viewed as negative—a black boy with no father in the home being raised by a single mother; they saw instead a loving, fiercely protective mama bear and a bright, curious boy who had been aching to step into his power. At Trinity, my child was finally free to express the fullness of who he knew himself to be. I felt liberated, too. For me, the church was a salve on the doubts that assailed me: *Are you doing right by Jordan? Can you really give him all that he needs?*

I now saw that, in fact, I could *not* give him everything he would require to grow into a strong, principled, courageous young black man in a country that would not always welcome him, but I had found a faith family that would fill in the gaps. At Trinity, the children's ministry was large and well organized. Jordan joined the Sunday school, where each age group received developmentally attuned instruction on Jesus's care for them, and guidance on how to engage their divine responsibility to be agents of God's love. The children also enjoyed popcorn parties, basketball camps, and spiritual retreats at which they played, read the scriptures, and bonded.

Since I was still flying most weekends, I could seldom attend Sunday services, so Jordan stayed over with the Maynard family and went to church with them. On Wednesday evenings, he and I would attend the weeknight service together and we'd have long conversations afterward about the lessons we'd heard.

"If God has all the power, why does he let people hurt each other?" Jordan asked one night while procrastinating over getting ready for bed.

"God has given us free will," I explained. "We learn our lessons best when we can experience them firsthand."

Jordan thought for a moment. "I don't need to get hurt or to hurt someone to know it feels bad," he said.

I circled his shoulders with my arm and pulled him close.

"God has his hand on you," I whispered.

"I'm special," he agreed. "That's because you prayed for me to be here."

I kissed his smooth brown forehead. "And God answered my prayers," I told him. "Now go to bed."

Over the years, these kinds of conversations with my son never struck me as unusual. Looking back now, I cannot help but wonder what Jordan knew.

———

Soon after joining Trinity, I transitioned my work schedule to weekday turnarounds—flying out and returning to Atlanta the same day—so I could attend Sunday services with Jordan. Some months, I didn't fly at all. Instead, I worked in the corporate office, interviewing and hiring flight attendants. I wanted to make sure that I could come home to Jordan every single day. I also enjoyed being able to participate in more activities at church. As a veteran of theater workshops and acting classes in my youth, I gravitated toward the drama ministry, auditioning for the role of Mary Magdalene in the Easter season passion play. I felt a kinship with the character of Mary, a woman cast off and alone, whom Jesus nevertheless deemed worthy of the full light of his love.

Perhaps it was the feeling of being so deeply sustained by the church that gave me the courage to transfer Jordan to a new school in the middle of his second-grade year. Things had not improved with his teacher, and so when two longtime friends from Delta encouraged me to enroll Jordan in a predominantly black Christian school in Atlanta that their own children attended, I decided to make the switch.

Jordan adjusted quickly, especially since he already knew the children of my fellow flight attendants Derrick Moite and Vernell Johnson. Our three families had been friends for almost a decade, and our children often played together at birthday parties and backyard barbecues. I was exclusively flying weekday turnarounds by then, with the security of knowing that Derrick or Vernell could always be counted on to pick Jordan up from school and keep him with them until my flight returned home. Derrick in particular became a loving father figure for Jordan, joining Conrad Maynard and Pastor Artis Crum as the primary African American male role models in his life. These three showed my son what it meant to be a proud, upstanding black man, one who lived his faith, cherished his spouse, and was devoted to his children. As Jordan grew older, he would spend more time with Ron in Jacksonville, and his dad would become a rock on whom he could depend. But back when he was six and seven years old, it was Derrick, Conrad, and Artis who willingly stepped into the surrogate father role.

It turned out that we'd need their and Ron's support more than we could have known. Not long after Jordan changed schools, I was diagnosed with stage one breast cancer, and referred for a lumpectomy and radiation. That experience completely transformed the way I would choose to mother Jordan going forward. It's why, at the end of Jordan's third-grade year, I decided to homeschool my son. Despite how much he was enjoying the black Christian school, I knew it was time to bring my boy home. *No more paper boats*, I thought, recalling the first-grade behavior chart. For the past three years our lives had felt as pasted together as that paper boat, but now I intended to help Jordan construct a good solid ship for the future.

CHAPTER 7

Love Again

CURTIS McBATH TURNED INTO MY driveway at precisely five in the morning to take me to the hospital. I'd made sure to schedule my procedure for a week when Jordan could be with his father in Jacksonville. Curtis and I had become friends on a three-day layover we'd flown together. It was like that with the people with whom you crewed. The forced togetherness of layovers was a powerful bonding experience. The entire flight crew would check into a hotel, change and freshen up in our rooms, and then meet back in the lobby to go out to eat. After dinner, we'd explore whatever city we were in, laughing and having a good time before heading back to the hotel to get a good night's sleep before the next morning's leg of the itinerary.

I especially enjoyed working on bigger aircrafts; the larger crews meant there would be at least a couple of people in the group I could relate to. Many fellow flight attendants became close friends not just on the job, but outside of work as well. Curtis was one of those friends of long standing. Solidly built with a handsome face and a warm, approachable manner, he'd been a patient listener when my mother had to be moved to a nursing home. Curtis invested in stocks and bonds on the side, and he'd advised me on how to shelter Mom's retirement income so that she'd have enough to cover her medical expenses. Our relationship, strictly platonic, felt like family.

As it worked out, Curtis wasn't scheduled to fly the day I was due to have my lumpectomy at Emory Hospital, and he'd offered to drive me to my appointment. He settled down in the waiting room as two nurses, one black, one white, escorted me to a room downstairs where a technician was to perform an ultrasound of my left breast. She would mark for the surgeon the exact area where the calcifications had been found. Before I entered a small cubicle to change into a hospital gown, one of the nurses touched my arm.

"Would it be okay if we prayed with you?" she asked. I nodded and reached for her hand, and we three made a small circle and bowed our heads. The nurse sent up a heartfelt petition for my healing as her coworker pressed a small beaded cross into my palm. Afterward, I hugged and thanked them both, full of wonder that I had been placed in the care of these prayer warriors.

A few minutes later I was lying on the exam table, clutching my little cross. I felt strangely peaceful, even when I saw the technician's brows draw together in a quizzical look. I smiled, already suspecting what was puzzling her.

I thought back to the day when I'd first learned I had breast cancer. Right in the little exam room, after the doctor had left, I got down on my knees and started praying. "Lord," I said, "I know this is not your will for me. I don't accept this diagnosis; I don't receive this, because I know you want me to raise my boy. I've got a long life to live and a lot of raising left to do. Jordan is your child, Lord, and I don't believe that you would entrust him to my care and then take me away from him."

That night, at Wednesday evening services, all the worshippers in attendance had circled me in prayer. They laid hands on me, and spoke in tongues. Then Yvette Maynard, who was a breast cancer survivor herself, placed her palm against my left breast, over my heart and toward my shoulder where I had told her the calcifications had been found. At her touch, a wave of heat shot through my entire body, and I started convulsing and retching, but nothing came up. I knelt there, gasping and shuddering as the people around me prayed. Suddenly, a sensation like a cold whoosh flooded through me, like cool brook water running through my veins, chasing the heat, and I felt cleansed and spiritually whole inside, and I knew I had been healed.

Two weeks later, as the ultrasound technician repositioned me on the table, her expression was concerned. I asked her what was wrong.

"I'm having a hard time locating the area of your cancer," she told me.

"Well, you probably won't find it because I've been healed," I said.

She paused and looked at me. "What do you mean?"

"I've been healed by God."

She turned back to the ultrasound machine. "I hope I don't have to prove you wrong," she muttered, almost to herself, as if she thought I might be slightly deranged. She adjusted my body for the umpteenth time and pressed the transducer against my left breast. She frowned at the sonogram screen as she maneuvered the probe.

"Go ahead and do whatever you have to," I said pleasantly, "but you won't find anything, because I've been healed. I just came here this morning because I know I have to follow medical protocol. But there won't be any surgery today. I'm sure of it."

The technician left the room to call my doctors, who kept me in the pre-op area for more than two hours, trying in vain to find the cancer that had been plain as day on my X-rays just two weeks before. Finally, they put down their diagnostic tools. "Mrs. Davis, we're going to send you back upstairs," my surgeon said. "I'm going to confer with the other doctors and we'll bring you back in six months to do these images again."

She didn't say: you don't have cancer. Her medical training wouldn't allow her to accept that. But I had no doubt whatsoever.

"Dr. Phillips, I can't thank you enough," I said. "You are one of the top female surgeons treating breast cancer in this country and I'm so grateful to have you as my physician. But you won't find anything in six months either. You've just witnessed a miracle. I know you can't admit that, but it's true."

She laughed, conceding nothing. "Six months," she said.

Meanwhile, the pre-op nurses were a-whooping and a-hollering as if we were at a revival meeting. "Thank you, Jesus! Praise God!" they exulted.

I slapped palms with them, then I got dressed and went to find Curtis.

"It's gone," I told him. "The cancer is completely gone. I can go home."

Six months later, my images once again came back clear, and my doctor pronounced me cancer-free. It was summer by then, and I was already making plans to homeschool Jordan in the fall.

—————

After so recently confronting my mortality, teaching Jordan would turn out to be, hands down, the most fulfilling experience of my life. The first year, fourth grade, it was just the two of us on the home-schooling journey. I had chosen a Board of Education–approved cur-riculum that I adjusted to accommodate Jordan's particular learning style. At eight years old, my son was an experiential learner. He had to touch, taste, see, feel, and hear a thing to truly internalize the knowledge. So we incorporated baseball stats into the math curriculum because he played Little League and loved the game. During our study of social justice movements, we'd huddle on the stairs and pore over photo albums of Jordan's grandparents at civil rights marches, then compare how seminal events like the march from Selma to Montgomery were portrayed in the black and white press of the time. We'd act out scenes from *Wind in the Willows* in the garden because Jordan had inherited my love of theater and he enjoyed being outside. We'd set up for our lessons in different places around the house, just to keep things interesting. Trips to San Diego, New York, and Chicago to visit family members would include some study of US geography, and wherever we traveled, we'd make it a point to visit regional art, science, and natural history museums.

Jordan was easy to parent, and entertaining to teach, because he wanted to see everything, do everything, know everything. I only had to say, "Let's go," and he'd be ready. I never had to push for or cajole his cooperation. But he asked *so many* questions. Sometimes he wore me out. Usually, I'd answer, "Well, Jordan, what do *you* think?" I was consciously training him to analyze the world around him critically. I didn't want him to swallow my thoughts and opinions whole; I wanted him to come up with his own. That meant we often had rousing discussions about the material we were studying, because my son was easily as opinionated as I was. I told him he should become a lawyer or perhaps an activist, because he had a love of debate and a gift for persuasion. His response was typical.

"God already knows what I'm going to do," he said.

When I started homeschooling Jordan, I had once again adjusted my work schedule. I was flying turnarounds only on weekends now, so that I could be home to teach during the week. But that meant I was essentially working seven days a week. In order to carve out a little "me time," for Jordan's fifth-grade year I decided to enroll him two days a week at the Home'sCool Depot, a community home-school support program affiliated with Trinity Chapel and a few other evangelical churches. Jordan, a naturally social boy, loved the idea and quickly began making new friends.

My only concern was that even though the congregation at Trinity was richly diverse, the Home'sCool Depot families were almost all white. The environment was scarcely integrated, and many days, Jordan was the only child of color in his group. Perhaps I was suffering from PTSD after my experience at his first school, or perhaps it was simply that I was raising a black boy in America, but I found myself bracing for racial incidents. There were a few: One day, for example, Jordan went to use the bathroom and while he was in there, a white girl from a younger group locked him inside the stall. When she finally let him out after many minutes, my son was crying, which only deepened his humiliation.

"Why did you lock me in?" he demanded of the girl.

"You're a monkey!" she yelled and ran away.

Jordan went straight to the teacher-mom on duty and reported what had happened, but the mom merely sent him to do an assignment, and said nothing to the girl. When I heard all this, I was incensed. I went into the Depot the next day to ask the teacher-mom why she hadn't spoken to the girl.

"Locking him in the bathroom was bad enough," I said, "but she called him a monkey. That's derogatory. You know what she meant."

The teacher-mom was sympathetic, and she promised to have a conversation with the girl. I suggested that perhaps she should also address the incident with the girl's parents, because the child was probably picking up on attitudes she had been exposed to at home. The teacher nodded, her expression suitably concerned.

That incident forced me to focus on the fact that most home-schooled children in America were from white evangelical Christian families, a large number of them politically conservative and racially insular. There weren't many liberal minority families homeschooling their kids, so it stood to reason that most of the teachers, parents, and children at the Depot didn't have a whole lot of experience interacting with black folks. I was determined that our troubles in Jordan's first-grade classroom would not be repeated. I believed that racism thrived in ignorance, and so I let go of the notion of "me time" and signed up to become a teacher-mom at the Depot on Tuesdays and Thursdays, the days Jordan was there. That way, I could keep a watchful eye on my boy and increase the other children's exposure to people who might be culturally different from them.

I was relieved to see that my worries about Jordan's standing with the homeschool kids were unfounded. The bathroom incident aside, Jordan had developed a tight-knit group of friends at the Depot, and he didn't hesitate to mix them in with the black kids who were his friends in our Douglasville neighborhood. He had also made close friends in the youth group at our church. My son was confidently navigating an integrated social circle, interacting with kids who were black, white, Asian, Native American, and Latino. I knew that his comfort within these diverse groups would serve him well as he grew to adulthood.

A natural leader and organizer, Jordan would pile his friends from the neighborhood into our car on Monday nights, and we'd head for the roller skating rink. Jordan would encourage the kids from the Depot to join us there. The kids would ask their parents if they could go skating because "Miss Lucia is going to be there, and she said she'll supervise us." In short order I became the Home'sCool Depot's official "skate mom," watching over Jordan and a rainbow of up to ten kids every Monday night at the rink.

———

Jordan was nine years old now, and, when he wasn't being homeschooled, he would spend time with his dad. We had developed a routine: Ron would fly to meet us at the Atlanta airport when I went to work, and he and Jordan would get on a plane and travel back to Jacksonville. Jordan spent some of his weekends plus a couple of weeks in the summer and part of the Christmas holidays there. As when Ron and I were first married, this commuting arrangement only worked because we had non-rev benefits as employees of the airline. But even though I was happy that Jordan was bonding more closely with his dad, he confessed he was lonely in Jacksonville. He had no friends his own age there, and felt out of his element. He preferred to be in Atlanta, riding his bike, playing with his dog, and hitting baseballs with his buddies from the neighborhood.

One of his best friends, an African American boy named Josiah, lived directly across our cul-de-sac. Among Jordan's other close friends were two white kids from the Home'sCool Depot, Charlie and Hunter. From the start, Charlie embraced my son as a brother, but Jordan and Hunter didn't start out in an amicable way. When they first encountered each other, Hunter would taunt Jordan and call him names. Jordan never responded. He'd just shrug and walk away, then later complain to me. My own assessment was that Hunter was an alpha boy jockeying for the attention of another alpha boy. Whatever it was, Hunter would continually try to verbally intimidate my son. Because Jordan was now old enough to fight his own battles I didn't intervene. Still, I wasn't above a little coaching. The next time Jordan grumbled to me about Hunter, I decided it was time for a heart talk, the kind where we popped up a big bowl of popcorn and sat together on the porch to discuss things.

"Listen, son, you have to let Hunter know it's not acceptable for him to talk to you like that," I told him. "If you think someone is demeaning you, then you have a right to defend yourself. You always have a right to defend who you are."

"You're saying I should fight him?" Jordan asked, wrinkling his forehead.

"No, absolutely not," I told him. "We're not talking about fighting. We're talking about standing up for yourself, and about the fact that you always have the right to be exactly who you are. You are a young black boy and no one should ever try to make you feel less than they are. If they try, then you defend your honor. You defend who you are."

"But why do I even need to defend who I am?" he said, exasperated. "Why should anybody treat me different or be mean to me just because I'm black?"

"You have to understand, Jordan, you are a very kind and loving person, and some people will take that as weakness. Now I'm not saying you need to change the way you are—not at all. But you need to defend who you are, verbally, not physically. You need to let people know you will not be disrespected. You will not be undermined."

"But I still don't get it," he said. "I'm always the one getting picked on and I'm not even doing anything!"

He paused.

"What's undermined?" he asked.

I found myself explaining to my nine-year-old, not for the first time, that there would always be white people in America who refused to believe that black people could be just like them. They would hold on to racist beliefs that black people were less intelligent, that our families were dysfunctional, and that we didn't raise our kids in church. "But what I need you to know is that you are no different than any white person," I told Jordan. "You're just as bright, just as intelligent, just as creative, just as strong, and you're just as entitled to everything the country of your birth has to offer. God made you every bit as special as any one of the kids you hang with, and don't let anybody tell you any differently. And I want you to defend yourself if you feel someone is trying to make you think otherwise."

He nodded, his expression solemn.

"One more thing," I added, cupping his face with my palm. "I've got your back and God has your back. Always."

The very next day, when Hunter came at Jordan in his usual taunting way, my son was ready. "You need to quit being such a bully," Jordan told him. "I'm not trying to fight you, Hunter. But I'm not afraid of you either."

This time, it was Hunter who walked away. He looked bemused. The next time I checked in with Jordan about how things were going with Hunter, he laughed and said, "Oh, we're friends now."

By the end of that school year, Jordan and Hunter had become inseparable, and they would remain that way till the day Jordan died. I have often wished that more of us could be like those two boys: we could learn so much from the way they transformed antagonism and suspicion into mutual respect and lasting brotherhood.

———

The phone was ringing. I saw on the caller ID that it was Curtis. I prepared to settle down for a long chat beside the upstairs dormer window, overlooking the cul-de-sac where Jordan and Josiah were dribbling a basketball. Curtis was in a hard place. He and his fiancée had recently broken up, and he'd turned to me for comfort.

"How's it going?" I answered brightly.

"Hey Lucy, do you scuba dive?" he asked, sounding more cheerful than I'd been expecting. "And if not, do you want to learn?" He launched into an explanation of how he'd bought tickets for a scuba diving excursion for himself and his ex, and he'd also purchased all the dive gear she might have needed. Rather than have it go to waste, maybe I'd like to go on vacation with him in his ex-fiancée's place?

"When's the trip?" I asked.

"July Fourth weekend. You in?"

"Why not?" I said. "I've scuba dived before. I'm not bad either."

Jordan was scheduled to spend the week of July Fourth in Jacksonville with his dad and his new wife, Carolina, so Curtis's invitation was well timed. As far as I was concerned, we were two friends heading to the beach for a good time. It was true that I found Curtis attractive, and I enjoyed his company, but romance was not on the agenda. All I cared about was raising Jordan up right, going to church, doing my job, and being there for my family and friends.

I certainly had no intention of marrying again, and so I didn't read anything but friendship into the fact that Curtis and I would talk on the phone for hours. And after our scuba vacation, when he invited me to run the Peachtree Road Race with him, it only made sense. He'd already bought tickets for his ex. Why let them go unused? He and I were both runners after all. As for all those times we went out to dinner, we were just two work pals who had traveled the globe, and who both happened to enjoy fine cuisine. And when Curtis had offered to take me to the hospital for the lumpectomy? Well, it was the sort of thing any good friend would do.

On June first of that year, I spent my birthday non-revving with Jordan to San Diego. He was to stay for two weeks at the beach with my sister, Lori, and his cousins. After handing my boy off to his aunt Lori at the airport, I turned right around and flew back to Atlanta the same day. I arrived home at nine that night, and was getting ready for bed when Curtis called.

"It's your birthday," he said. "Let me take you out to dinner."

As I so often found myself saying to Curtis these days, I answered, "Why not?"

We went to the Cheesecake Factory the following evening. Over dessert, Curtis sat back in his chair, just looking at me.

"What's up," I said, lifting a forkful of brownie cheesecake to my lips.

"We should do this more often," he said.

"Do what? We're eating."

"Well, we're on a date."

"This isn't a date," I scoffed. "We're just friends."

"Well, I'd like us to change that," Curtis said.

I put down my fork.

"Are you *serious*?"

"As a heart attack," he confirmed.

And that is how Curtis McBath and I officially became a couple. Still, I didn't introduce him to Jordan as the man I was dating for eighteen months more. And as I anticipated, when I did, it was challenging.

———

Jordan, now on the cusp of adolescence, wasn't as easy to predict or manage as he had previously been. Part of it was the simple fact that he was getting older, but I suspected some of it had to do with suddenly having to share my attention. It had always been just Jordan and me, and now I was asking him to welcome Curtis into our family time. Jordan had never seen me with a man other than his father before, and he didn't like it one bit.

I hadn't anticipated that Jordan would be so rude to Curtis, sullen and uncommunicative. When Curtis tried to engage him by talking about a baseball game on television or asking him about his friends, Jordan would mumble, "You're not my father," and walk away. I didn't have to be a therapist to figure out that he hoped his surly behavior might drive Curtis away. He was wrong. Curtis turned out to be made of more stubborn stuff. I loved his kindness toward my son, and his optimism that in time Jordan would warm to him. Yet when he proposed marriage the first time, I turned him down. "You need to spend more time embracing my child," I told him. "You don't know our routines. You have no idea what it's like to suddenly have to fold yourself in to a ready-made family. I know Jordan's been difficult, but we're the grown-ups here. We have to find a way to help him feel secure."

Jordan, Curtis, and I all worked to reach a common understanding of our place in each other's lives. I prayed constantly that Curtis and Jordan would find a way to be friends. I wasn't looking for a new father for my boy—he already had one who was completely devoted to him—but I did want the two most important people in my life to cut each other some slack. And over time, my prayers began to be answered. Curtis and Jordan would watch Sunday afternoon ballgames together, and on occasion even play video games in the den. As the two of them grew more comfortable with each other, I started to consider what it might be like to marry again. Curtis had proposed to me four times by then, and every time I'd said no. But my love for him had only grown deeper, and now I began to think seriously about what life might be like with this good and decent man, who was not only a wonderful romantic partner but was also my best friend. I prayed for guidance. "Lord," I whispered, "please let me know if this is your will."

The next time Curtis broached the idea of getting married, I said yes.

On October 18, 2008, my handsome son walked me down the aisle toward the man who would become his stepfather. At the center of my happiness was a kernel of sober recognition that this was the end of an era for Jordan and me, and not just because we were remaking our little family. The plan was to sell our house in Douglasville and for both of us to move into Curtis's larger home in Marietta, a racially inclusive, middle-class suburb of Atlanta. Our homeschooling journey would also be at an end. Jordan would enter ninth grade at Marietta High School the following year.

As Curtis and I said our "I do's," sweeping changes were also taking place on the national political landscape. Less than a month later, on the historic night of November 4, 2008, Jordan, Curtis, and I gathered in the den to watch as President-elect Barack Obama, with his beautiful wife and daughters nearby, gave a stirring victory speech from Grant Park in Chicago. I wished my parents had been alive to see this moment, the culmination of all they worked for in their lifetimes, the triumph of hope and courage over bigotry and fear. The new president was, for me, a powerful affirmation that bright, motivated, socially conscious African American boys like my Jordan could grow up to be anything they chose, so long as they were willing to work hard, dream big, and refuse to let doubt and fear turn them aside.

PART TWO

LOUD MUSIC

CHAPTER 8

Fast Traps

MOST AFRICAN AMERICANS CAN REMEMBER exactly where they were on the evening of January 3, 2008, when they learned that Barack Obama had won the Iowa Democratic Presidential Caucus. In the freezing American heartland, in one of the whitest states in the nation, the black Democratic candidate posted his first victory of the 2008 presidential campaign. It hadn't mattered that 93 percent of the state's Democratic caucus goers were white. Those voters had seen something in the lean, erudite senator, his accomplished wife, and well-mannered daughters as they traveled from one end of the state to the other, canvassing for support. The first-term US senator's unabashed belief in a less divided America had stirred hope in their prairie hearts. With a decisive turnout, Iowa Democrats cast their lot with Obama.

I was in my kitchen cooking dinner when the announcement came over the television that the candidate from my home state of Illinois had prevailed.

"He won!" I called out to Jordan, who was watching an NBA basketball game in the next room. "Barack Obama won in Iowa!"

"That's great!" Jordan yelled back, but I knew from his automatic tone that this victory was not nearly as momentous for him as it was for me. He didn't understand just how outrageous it was to consider that a black man could actually become the nation's commander-in-chief. Ironically, I'd raised Jordan to believe that he could do and be anything, even president of the United States; his complexion should never be viewed as a barrier to success, even if he might have to work twice as hard as a white peer to achieve his dreams. So for Jordan, Obama's win on that cold January night was merely proof of what I had been preaching his entire life. He was happy, but not astounded.

I, on the other hand, found the victory transformative. I felt an electric jolt of possibility, because the Iowa win was unequivocal proof that Obama had a real chance at the White House. But as I turned back to preparing dinner, I became aware of a low-grade current of anxiety weaving through my joy. Would America really allow a black man to win the presidency? Would his Secret Service detail be vigilant enough to ward off the inevitable threats to his life?

"I almost hope he doesn't win," an elderly Jamaican woman at church had told me just the Sunday before, clutching my hands in hers. "I'm afraid they'll shoot him."

"Oh, Ms. Gloria," I'd said, hugging her. "We can't let fear hold us back from making real progress."

She was still dubious. "You know, I pray for him like he's my own son," she said. "I hope you're praying, too. That young man needs our prayers." She patted my hand, then planted her cane and shambled away.

Now, alone in my kitchen, I felt a twinge of the same worry that had preoccupied her and so many others. We were a nation with a long history of destroying black men, especially those who dared greatly.

We'd all seen the pictures of black bodies swinging from southern trees, a mob of southern whites cheering below. Contrary to what many believed, the lynching never ended. Instead it had morphed into one unarmed black man after another being gunned down in the streets—by law enforcement, by white vigilantes, by street gangs in neighborhoods fractured by poverty, drugs, crime. In a nation where almost anybody could lay hands on a firearm, black men were fourteen times more likely to be shot and killed than white men.[1] Given the racial climate, could a candidate like Barack Obama ever feel safe?

I recalled the *60 Minutes* interview that veteran CBS reporter Steve Kroft had conducted with Barack and Michelle Obama one year before.[2] The segment had aired one day after the forty-five-year-old senator's February 10, 2007, announcement that he would seek the presidency. At one point in the interview, after a series of lighthearted exchanges, Kroft turned serious. "This is a tough question to ask," he said, addressing the senator's wife. "But a number of years ago [former secretary of state] Colin Powell was thinking about running for president. His wife, Alma, really did not want him to run because she was worried about some crazy person with a gun. Has that been a factor? I mean, have you talked about that? Is that something that you think about?"

Michelle Obama didn't flinch. "I don't lose sleep over it," she said, "because the realities are that as a black man, Barack could get shot going to the gas station. You can't make decisions based on fear and the possibility of what might happen. We just weren't raised that way."

I thought: *If Michelle can put the steel in her back and support her husband stepping onto the world's largest stage, the least I can do is believe in our collective prayers to see him through.*

But my heart was heavy. Even a Harvard-educated attorney,

born and raised in Hawaii, transplanted to Chicago, Illinois, who had never been in trouble with the law, who had himself been a professor of law before running for US senator, even this man had to reckon with the fact that he would forever be a target simply because he walked through the land of his birth in black skin. I tried to banish such thoughts, because I was trying to raise a proud, ambitious young black man myself. And Lord knows, I intended to keep him safe.

Of course, I had no clue then that my son's life would be cut short by an angry man's bullet less than three months before his eighteenth birthday. At the time I gave little thought to the manner in which the gun lobby was, even then, race-baiting conservative evangelical Christians and white supremacists who didn't hold with the notion that black folks could and should ascend to the same heights as whites. Even before the nation successfully elected a black man as president, the Political Victory Fund of the National Rifle Association was already using his race and progressive platform as a recruitment and fundraising tool for the organization.

As a candidate, Obama had repeatedly assured the country that he supported the Second Amendment, yet the NRA insisted in tens of thousands of brochures mailed to right-wing voters that "Barack Obama would be the most anti-gun president in American history." They went so far as to call the president-to-be a liar: "When it comes to your Second Amendment rights, he refuses to speak honestly about where he stands."[3]

In response, rural white nationalists and Christian evangelicals flocked to gun shows in warehouses bigger than a football field, buying weapons by the millions. According to the *Journal of Public Economics*, federal tax receipts from the sale of firearms increased 90 percent in the twelve-month period before Obama was elected, with the demand for firearms rising by 60 percent immediately after his election. Even though the number of Americans who owned firearms stood at 43 percent, down a few points from the peak gun ownership years of the mid-1990s,[4] the quantity and variety of weapons being sold was exploding, with an unprecedented 23 million firearm permits issued in 2015 alone.[5] In fact, for every year that Barack Obama was president, the tally of guns sold in America rose, prompting the *U.S. News and World Report* to proclaim "the Obama Effect," suggesting "the NRA Should Send Obama a 'Thank You' Card."[6]

"Trust God, but not man," say many evangelicals who insist their gun rights are being threatened. They give a knowing smirk as they pat their firearms. This is usually code for a rampant distrust of those who, in their view, are not like them, the black and brown people, the criminals, illegals, and terrorists, the inner-city poor, and all those whom the NRA's leaders aggressively and repetitively warn will be coming for the "good" Americans' homes and families. It turns out that instilling a globalized fear of "the other" has been a wildly successful marketing ploy for the NRA. Using dog whistle racial language such as the words *urban*, *animals*, and *thugs*—while also hammering home the notion of *we* and *they*—the organization's leadership has inflamed ancient hatreds buried deep in America's heart.

One researcher set out to determine if Obama's race had directly influenced the frenzy of gun buying among whites. For each state in which the sale of firearms had skyrocketed due to the so-called Obama Effect, he measured the state's level of racial animus by analyzing Google data for racially discriminatory search terms. When he compared the two charts, he found an unmistakable correlation.[7]

During Obama's time in office, anecdotal evidence of this racial animosity abounded. In the summer of 2014, for example, amid protests in Ferguson, Missouri, sparked by the fatal shooting of Michael Brown, an unarmed black teen who took six bullets for defying a cop's demand that he stop jaywalking, NRA board member Ted Nugent posted on Facebook what he claimed was a list of white people killed by black people. He provided no sourcing for any of the cases, none of which had been reported in the news. Nugent's true intent was transparent: he aimed to give the impression that whites needed to arm themselves against a widespread threat from black people.

As billions poured into the treasure chests of gun manufacturers following Obama's win, the stock prices of major gun companies rose, and the number of retail gun dealers increased for the first time in two decades. The US gun lobby was rolling in cash, with the NRA reporting some $24 million in its coffers two years into Obama's first term. With no evidence whatsoever to point to—except perhaps Obama's appointment of two Supreme Court justices who supported sensible gun laws—the gun lobby continued to claim that Obama was hostile to the Second Amendment and would certainly repeal it if he won a second term. "Gun owners and hunters fear that a second Obama administration with no future political campaigns to worry about will try to destroy this great American freedom," a spokesman for the NRA declared.[8]

The group's Political Victory Fund underscored this message during Obama's 2012 bid for reelection: "If Barack Obama wins a second term in office, our Second Amendment freedom will not survive," their mailing brochures asserted. "Obama will never have to face the voters again, and will therefore be unleashed to push the most extreme elements of his gun-ban agenda to every corner of America."[9]

It is a great source of comfort to me that despite dog whistle tactics designed to inflame white voters, America nevertheless returned Barack Obama to office by an even larger margin than he won in 2008. To me, this means the gun lobby's divisive and misleading propaganda was not then, and is not now, being swallowed whole by the nation's fifty-five million gun owners,[10] including the NRA's chief demographic, white evangelical Christians. Given that estimates of evangelicals in the US population have run as high as 47 percent, with the vast majority identifying as Republican, Obama's second term suggests to me that gun safety advocates and pro-gun Christians might yet be able to find some common ground.

———

Even though in 2010 I was still relatively uninformed of the threat that America's lenient gun laws posed to its citizens, I was certainly conscious of the frequent police shootings of unarmed black men. This tragic circumstance was in part fueled by a long-standing American stereotype of black criminality, a label applied to the universe of African American men since Reconstruction. Back then, as whites sought to contain black progress by relegating newly freed blacks to a lower social rung than white citizens, law enforcement overly policed our communities, often arresting black men on false or trumped up charges. Social scientists then used African Americans' disproportionate arrest and incarceration records as evidence of Negro pathology and inferiority. These "facts" became the justification for racial exclusion from avenues of social advancement, as well as for the continued use of excessive police force against and mass incarceration of black men in the name of public safety.

Many whites still believe that African Americans' challenging social and economic circumstances are proof of their lesser character and lifestyle. They cite the example of other poor and ghettoized groups, the Jews, the Irish, and the Italians, who were able to lift themselves out of poverty in a generation. Their comparison ignores the fact that these voluntary immigrants could become "anonymously white" as they accessed channels of social mobility, while blacks were always visible to the forces that sought to subjugate them. Perhaps the tactic that most severely limited the advancement of African Americans was the banking practice of redlining black neighborhoods, effectively denying us mortgages and home loans. As a result, African Americans were systematically locked out of the nation's primary tool for building generational wealth: home ownership.

This state of affairs remained mostly the case all the way up until 1988, when my hometown paper, the *Atlanta Journal-Constitution*, published a four-part exposé called "The Color of Money."[11] The series revealed rampant discrimination in mortgage lending locally and across the country, a pattern of excluding blacks that stretched back many decades. Although mortgage lenders were subsequently forced to extend credit to African Americans, our families and our communities are still trying to make up financial ground. It's why so many of us still languish in poverty, eking out an existence in depressed, crime-ridden urban neighborhoods where confrontations with police happen on a regular basis, and can be deadly.

I had tried to shield Jordan from all that. And yet, like every parent of a black boy, I knew deep down that a bullet sped by America's ancient racial story could one day take my son from me. All parents of African American sons live with this knowledge, and we pray that we will never be asked to endure our child's final breath. But, even as we send up petitions for our children's safety, and work to change the structural racism that puts them in jeopardy, we must also focus on helping them live joyfully and purposefully above the daily micro- and macro-aggressions that are a constant in their lives. Jordan's father and I were keenly aware that as our son grew older, we needed to prepare him to navigate the world as a young black man, powerful and proud, yet without the bitterness and anger that would corrode his own heart. As James Baldwin put it more than half a century ago in *Notes of a Native Son*, "The fight begins . . . in the heart, and it now had been laid to my charge to keep my own heart free of hatred and despair."[12]

Even if Baldwin had guessed that almost six decades later his words would still apply so fully, I doubt he'd have anticipated the relentless hail of police bullets snuffing out young black lives. One explanation offered by social scientists for the combustible relationship between some (not all) white cops and African American boys is that many white cops live in social worlds that are almost entirely segregated, and so when they encounter black boys, they meet them as strangers. They do not see reflections of their younger brothers, cousins, children, neighbors, and friends. They do not see anyone with whom they are familiar in their personal lives, and they may not even recognize they are confronting a mere child.

One revealing study published in the *Journal of Personality and Social Psychology* examined the difference in how black and white children are treated based solely on race, in an effort to measure the degree to which black children are "dehumanized" in the eyes of different groups, including police officers.[13] "Children in most societies are considered to be in a distinct group with characteristics such as innocence and the need for protection," explained Dr. Phillip Atiba Goff, cofounder and president of the Center for Policing Equity at John Jay College of Criminal Justice in New York City. "Our research found that black boys can be seen as responsible for their actions at an age when white boys still benefit from the assumption that children are essentially innocent."[14]

While all respondents in the study overestimated the age of young black boys, the 60 police participants, mostly white males, who were asked to estimate the age of child crime suspects had the widest spread of all, judging black boys over the age of ten as 4.59 years older than their actual ages. A corresponding analysis of 116 police officers' on-the-job histories showed that a mistaken assessment of age factored into the greater use of force against black children as compared to white children in situations where the children were accused of similar crimes.[15] In other words, a white cop might see a black thirteen-year-old playing with a toy gun in a park, and he might assume the child to be an eighteen-year-old gangster about to open fire. He draws his weapon before he investigates, because in his split-second judgment the child has been dehumanized—seen as older and less innocent than a white child of the same age.

This study demonstrates why it is essential that black parents talk to their children about how they should conduct themselves in encounters with the police. Black parents call this "The Talk," the hopefully life-preserving conversation we dare not neglect having. But the conversation can be a tricky one.

To begin with, Ron and I felt it was important to raise Jordan to be proud of who he was, to stand up for his beliefs, to speak out about anything he saw as inappropriate or wrong, and to champion and protect other people as well as himself. I knew we were succeeding in getting these messages across, because Jordan, always a leader in his social group, was also a very mindful caretaker of his friends. It's why I thought he'd grow up to be a social activist, because I'd watched him bring people together, always consciously looking out for "the least of these" as Jesus himself put it in Matthew 25:35–40, one of my favorite biblical passages:

> "For I was hungry and you gave me food, I was thirsty and
> you gave me drink, I was a stranger and you welcomed me, I
> was naked and you clothed me, I was sick and you visited me,

I was in prison and you came to me." Then the righteous will answer him, saying, "Lord, when did we see you hungry and feed you, or thirsty and give you drink? And when did we see you a stranger and welcome you, or naked and clothe you? And when did we see you sick or in prison and visit you?" And the King will answer them, "Truly, I say to you, as you did to one of the least of these my brothers, you did to me."

In this sense, Jordan was doing God's work simply by how he lived, in the everyday choices he made, in the way he cared for his friends. Jordan wanted to make sure that the latchkey kids in the neighborhood had a place to come to after school where they could find company and nurture. I ended up having to buy an SUV just so I could fit all his friends in my car, because Jordan was always piling in one more. "Mom, we've got to take Ernie with us to the skating rink this week because if we don't he'll never get to go," he'd tell me. "Ernie's parents can't afford to do the things with him that you do with me."

That was Jordan, bridge builder, party planner, the one who folded everyone in, the nerds, the jocks, the awkward shy ones, Jordan befriended them all. Even boys who were two or three grades ahead of him were hanging out in my home, with Jordan always at the center of things. I used to joke with them, "Why are you listening to Jordan? What is it about him? You have more years on this earth than he does." They'd just laugh and shrug, because they knew, as I knew, that Jordan had a generous heart. He wanted all his friends to have what he had, which is why he was always bringing them to my kitchen for me to feed them. Whether it was pizza or Popsicles, Jordan would never take a portion for himself until everyone else was served. And he had a wisdom and comfort with himself that others found irresistible. People felt whole in his presence.

But even as Ron and I encouraged our son to express these qualities of leadership and care, as African American parents we needed to help him balance his sense of personal agency with the ability to strike the right tone when confronted by a police officer with a gun on his hip. How to convey to our boy that deference in this situation was not tantamount to submission; it would not diminish him. Rather, it would keep him alive, because one could never be quite sure of the mental tapes about people of color that might be playing in the mind of the police officer, whether he was aware of them or not.

It's the old unconscious bias story, because at the level of individuals (though not of institutions), racism in America has largely morphed into this difficult-to-challenge form. And nowhere is this subliminal stereotyping more deadly than in interactions between young black men and the police. So how do we prepare our children, especially our boys, to survive such interactions? African American psychologist Goff offers some insight. Goff's research on race and policing examines how racial contextual cues can lead to devastating outcomes, even absent overt racial hostility.

"One of the most common concerns that parents of successful non-dominant group kids have is how do I keep my babies safe while they are trying to do the right thing in a world that can feel as if it's lined up against their success," Goff says. "How do I keep them safe in a space that is not used to them or that might be afraid of them?"[16]

Goff breaks down how interracial encounters can sometimes play out. "The way that we think about racism is that bad people do it," he says. "We think it's some part of the contaminated heart or the contaminated mind, that you have racism somewhere in your soul and then it externalizes. When I go and I talk to kids and teachers and law enforcement about how racism happens, they say people have stereotypes, people have prejudices, and they act on it. And that's one way it happens. But this kind of explicit bias is not the only thing going on. There are other traps that are potentially more deadly."

Unconscious bias is one of the traps. Goff calls it a fast trap: thoughts happen quickly, below consciousness. "Now if what a police officer is thinking happens to be a stereotype, it can have deadly consequences, especially in a culture that associates black with criminal, Latino with illegal, Muslim with terrorism, and queer with predatory," he observes. "If you're a cop you might pull the trigger faster, because you're quicker to think your life is being threatened. And the terrible thing is that because these thoughts are happening beneath awareness, we are unable to engage with them and correct them directly."

The second type of trap, Goff explains, is a slow trap: this is when you're aware that a negative stereotype about your group is being applied to you. You're aware that the slow trap is happening, but you can't predict the consequences. In encounters with police, "this can provoke anxiety and deplete us cognitively," Goff says. Thoughts whirl in our brains: *Do they think I'm a criminal just because I'm black? Do I have to worry about my safety? What should I do with my hands?* Meanwhile, the officer is listening to his own mental tape: *Is this person a criminal? Do they think I'm a racist? I don't want to be seen as a racist but I also want to stay safe.*

"In this scenario, we don't make eye contact, we don't hear what the other person is saying, or we interpret it in terms of our own anxiety," Goff says. "And the results can be deadly. Yet none of these responses is the fault of the young black kid. As much as we want to protect our children, it's not their fault when other people hate or are suspicious of them before they ever meet them. So it's really important for us to say, you are not responsible for other people's feelings about you, especially if they harbored those feelings before you ever showed up."

His point is that we do our children a disservice when, out of a desire to protect them, we give them the message that they are answerable for how other people react to them. "We must explain to our children that other people's stories about you belong to them," he says. "They do not belong to you, and it's not your job to fix them. But it's important to be aware of the stories that are out there. And if we're concerned about what could happen to us, we can make smart decisions in negotiating other people's stories.

"What I mean by that is when you see law enforcement, understand that their job is to make you small so that they can be safe. So even if you feel that they are disrespectful of you, always say sir or ma'am, keep your hands where they can see them, and do exactly what they're asking, because their story is you can at any point in time get a weapon and hurt them. And if that is the story they are telling themselves, then you want to make a smart decision based on that."[17]

The most critical thing, Goff stresses, is to come out of the situation still breathing, even if the police officer is in the wrong. As long as you're alive, he notes, you can press charges later.

Sadly, while we knew to discuss with Jordan how best to survive a police interaction, it never occurred to us to rehearse just how he should behave if confronted by an incensed civilian with a handgun in the glove compartment of his car.

CHAPTER 9

A Hard Choice

RIGHT AROUND THE TIME JORDAN became a sophomore at Marietta High, our family's well-oiled routine hit a speed bump. Eight years after my first breast cancer diagnosis and miraculous healing, a malignancy had returned. This time when I went in for my lumpectomy, the calcifications were right there on the X-ray, bright white spots that looked like somebody had spattered bleach on the gray film.

"Okay, Lord," I said, "I'm ready to meet this trial."

The good Lord took me at my word, because over the next year everything I held most dear would be tested. First, my health: two months after the first lumpectomy, more calcifications were found, necessitating a second surgery and several weeks of radiation. I was exhausted all the time, and definitely not up to the task of engaging a teenager who was right at the developmental stage of pushing against boundaries. Curtis, seeing how debilitated the cancer treatments left me, tried to step in and help me parent my son. But when he talked to Jordan about taking responsibility for his assigned chores—vacuuming his room, cleaning his bathroom, walking the dog, laundering his clothes—Jordan was uncooperative. "He's not my father," he grumbled to me, a sentiment I hadn't heard from him since before Curtis and I were married. "Why's he suddenly trying to tell me what to do?"

I found myself playing referee. To Jordan, I'd say, "Well, son, Curtis knows that I'm sick right now and really not able to pick up your slack, so he's rightfully asking you to pull your weight." Meanwhile, late at night in bed, I'd say to Curtis, "I know your intentions are good, but don't try to be Jordan's dad. Let me deal with him myself." Curtis resented me trying to block his efforts to get Jordan to straighten up and fly right, just as Jordan resented me telling him that Curtis had a point. Nobody was happy. To make matters worse, Jordan was scared.

"Mom, I hate that you're sick," he said one afternoon, throwing himself onto the bed next to me like he used to do when he was little. He lay on his back and stared at the ceiling as he confessed his darkest fear. "What am I going to do if you die?"

"Oh, Jordan, I'm not going to die. I'm getting better. You'll see."

"But this is the second time you've had cancer," he said. "I didn't really get it the first time, I was too young, but now I know what it means."

"Look, son, if anything happens to me you still have your dad."

"But I don't want to live with Dad," he whined. "You promised me I wouldn't have to live in Jacksonville. You said I could always stay with you. I need you to get better, Mom. I need you to be okay."

I had indeed assured him that I'd never send him away. He had demanded it, after spending some weeks with his dad and his wife, Carolina, the summer before. Ron had lately started asking me to let Jordan come and live with him in Jacksonville. "A boy needs his father to show him how to be a man," he insisted, "and Jordan's getting to that stage." He had mentioned the idea to Jordan as well. But Jordan had been lonely for his friends and his life back in Atlanta, and didn't welcome the idea of a change. The first night he came home, he sat across from me at the kitchen counter and said, "Mom, promise me I can always live in Atlanta. I want to stay here with you."

"You sure can," I'd said, but my tone was too casual for his liking.

"Mom, promise me," he insisted. "Say, 'I promise.'"

"Well, Jordan," I said more seriously, "only God knows what is in store for me, but I promise you, I have no intention of sending you away. Yes, you can stay right here with me."

If only that assurance had been enough to smooth over the turbulence ahead. Curtis continued to fuss at Jordan for the chores he left undone, and frankly, my son's dismissive attitude about his responsibility to the household was getting to me, too. Then Jordan started testing our resolve about his 8 PM curfew. It wasn't anything too dramatic, just normal fifteen-year-old acting out, such as coming in at thirty minutes past the time we'd agreed he should be back in the house on weekday evenings. I was so wiped out from my surgeries and follow-up treatment, I didn't have the energy to argue. It was easier on some days to just let things slide. And yet I knew that without my intervention, the resentment between Jordan and Curtis might deepen and become more difficult to walk back. My son's rebellious adolescent behavior had caught Curtis off guard, and he wanted more than anything else to protect me. I tried to explain all this to Jordan, but I wasn't getting through.

"Just get better, Mom," he'd say. "I just need you to be well. Everything will be okay when you're not sick anymore." He sounded almost angry, but I knew it was fear. He looked like a young man now, and perhaps he thought he was too grown up to show just how scared he was feeling.

One July afternoon, in between bouts of radiation, I felt well enough to do the laundry. Curtis was at work, and Jordan had left the house earlier that morning to shoot hoops with Josiah and Davis, two of his neighborhood friends. I unloaded a pile sheets and towels from the dryer and carried them into the den. I turned on CNN, settled myself on the couch, and began sorting and folding as I caught up on the news.

I saw that out in California, a verdict had been delivered in the trial of the Bay Area cop accused of killing a twenty-two-year-old African American man on a train platform on New Year's Day 2009. I remembered the shooting well. Oscar Grant had been unarmed. He and his friends had been heading home from the previous night's festivities when an altercation broke out in the train car in which they were traveling. At the next stop, police swarmed onto the train. They pulled several young black men out of the car and subdued them on the platform of the BART Fruitvale station. Oscar Grant was lying facedown on the ground, restrained by two police officers, when one of them shot him in the back. The officer later claimed he meant only to use his Taser on Grant, but had drawn his handgun instead. I thought: *You had him facedown on the ground, two of you holding him. You didn't need to kill that poor boy. You didn't even need to Taser him.*

But the jurors had bought his defense. They judged him guilty of involuntary manslaughter instead of second-degree murder. Outside the courtroom after the verdict was read, the camera zoomed in on Oscar Grant's mother, her face a mask of dismay. "My son was murdered," she told a reporter later. "He was murdered. He was murdered. My son was murdered." She kept repeating it, as if to reclaim the truth she knew from the story now being told. I wanted to put my arms around her. I couldn't imagine what it must feel like to know that your child had been shot in the back while restrained on the ground, and then be told it was an accident.

I clicked off the television. It was suddenly too much. Right then, I heard Jordan coming through the front door, and my whole body loosened. I realized for the first time, and with a small sense of shock, that whenever my now teenage son walked out the door without me, I unconsciously tensed up, waiting for him to return home safely. Did every black parent in America feel this way?

I called out to Jordan and he came into the den. I pushed a pile of freshly laundered towels toward him.

"Help me fold," I said.

"I can't, Mom, I'm heading right back out. Josiah is waiting for me."

"Jordan—"

But he had already turned on his heel and was running up the stairs to his room. A minute later I heard him skip back down the stairs and slam the front door behind him. He was gone, and I didn't even know where. I wasn't too worried, because he was with Josiah, a gentle giant of a boy, a kind-hearted soul who was never in any kind of trouble. Still, Jordan had flouted yet another house rule, because he knew he was supposed to let me know where he would be at all times. Nor was he to simply *tell* me he was going out, he was supposed to ask if he *could*.

I sat unmoving on the couch long after Jordan blew into the house and then out again. Even though I sensed he was asserting his independence in a completely age-appropriate way, I still felt as if I had lost control. Perhaps all parents feel this way at some point during the teenage years. Or maybe Jordan was flirting with the idea that he might have to fly solo if anything happened to me. Whatever was going on, all I could think was: *How will I keep my boy safe if I can't make him stand still and listen to me?* How would I make him understand that a suburban street could be a dangerous place for a black boy doing nothing more than living his life? Did he truly know that in all things, he would have to be twice as good, twice as vigilant, and twice as aware of his actions? What if a fight broke out near him, and he got swept up in the melee as Oscar Grant did? What if he ran into a rogue cop, or a scared one? How could I make Jordan understand that as grown as he thought he was, he wasn't invulnerable?

For the first time in all my years of raising him, I began to wonder if he might need a firmer hand, a man's baritone in his ear, his father's influence. Ever since Jordan turned thirteen, Ron had been chafing to have his son come and live with him, but every time he asked, I reflexively said no. *No, no, no.* If I'm honest, I felt threatened by the idea of sending Jordan to his father. I feared I would lose my status as the favored parent.

Understand that for me, Jordan was the one person in my life who I believed loved me unconditionally. In the years after Ron and I broke up, I'd felt completely abandoned, especially when he moved back to Jacksonville and remarried. What saved me was raising Jordan, and the need to be whole and positive for him. Sometimes, it had felt like Jordan and me against the world. Even though God had indeed brought us a village of loyal friends who became a surrogate family, in terms of blood, it was still just Jordan and me in Atlanta. I had given myself completely to the task of mothering him, of giving him an upbringing that in no way lacked what two-parent families could provide for their children.

But the fact was, Jordan had another parent, and that parent was asking to be more involved. Perhaps it was time to allow Ron to be a full-time father to our son. No sooner than the thought floated to the surface of my mind, God breathed his guidance into the still, quiet air: *Let him go.*

I didn't make the call to Ron right away. I wanted to wait and see whether things got better after my radiation treatments ended. But I hadn't counted on how drained and worn out I'd feel by the time I was once again cancer-free. As I tried to regain my strength, I had little tolerance for the impertinent tone Jordan would sometimes take with Curtis and even with me. "If you are going to be disrespectful of this household, you're going to have to go and live with your father," I warned him. Things would change for a while, and then he'd regress, which of course is the way it often is with teenagers.

Ron's older son Ronnie, who was now married and working in law enforcement in Virginia, stayed in contact with Jordan during this time. The brothers had always been close, with Jordan texting Ronnie for advice about girls, and sometimes about dealing with his new family situation. Ronnie, who had called me Mom ever since his dad and I married, and even after we were divorced, encouraged Jordan to talk out his feelings with me. But Jordan had become reticent; I suspect he didn't want to admit just how anxious he still was about my recovery. I was grateful for Ronnie's presence in his life. It was a comfort to know that Jordan could rely on the brother who'd teasingly nicknamed him "Giraffe" when he stretched past six feet tall. In return, Jordan referred to Ronnie, who was shorter in stature, as "Little Big Brother."

Watching how Jordan allowed himself to be calmed by Ronnie, I grew increasingly convinced that my son needed the steadying hand of a man he trusted, and who better than his father, the man who loved him best. Finally, on a day when Jordan and I had an escalating argument over something so mundane as his forgetting to feed the dog, I calmly picked up the phone and dialed Ron's number.

"It's time," I told him.

Ron was ecstatic at the news. "Finally!" he exulted. "You just focus on getting better, Lucy. Rest easy that you've done everything you needed to do for Jordan. Now it's time for his father to transition him into manhood. I'll finish raising our boy."

We agreed Jordan would finish out the fall term in Marietta, and move to Jacksonville to live with Ron and Carolina in January. That would give Ron time to get him enrolled in a school there, and Jordan time to say goodbye to his friends.

The day Ron drove up from Jacksonville to pick Jordan up is seared in my memory. It was a chilly afternoon, a little more than a month before Jordan's sixteenth birthday. Curtis had left that morning to work a three-day international trip to Amsterdam. Back home in Marietta, my son was frostily silent. He didn't look at or speak to me as he stuffed the last of his clothes into his denim duffel, packed up his Xbox 360, gathered his favorite sneakers, and dumped the pile next to the front door. His friends Josiah, Hunter, Charlie, and Davis had slept over the night before, which was nothing new. There were always teenagers sleeping on my couch, on Jordan's floor, or in the den. Today, I was especially grateful for their presence; their joshing, backslapping boyishness siphoned off some of the hurt and anger Jordan was clearly feeling toward me.

I understood that he felt betrayed, and that in his mind, I was breaking a promise, and yet I believed that the time had come for him to go and live with his father. He was halfway through the tenth grade. He had two more years in high school, and if his dad was to have any part in the day-to-day raising of him, it was now or never. I knew that Ron's house rules were a little more stringent than mine—Jordan's curfew time was earlier in Jacksonville, his phone and video game rules stricter—and I thought that might be just what our son needed. Still, my own heart was in shreds as I processed the reality that he would be living away from me.

By the time Ron arrived at noon, the mood among the boys had turned somber. The teasing banter had quieted, and I saw that Jordan had tears in his eyes. I went to hold him, but he twisted away, and I let him be. I felt so helpless as I watched him greet his dad, and then swing his duffel into the back of Ron's black Highlander. The other boys carried the rest of his things and deposited them in the back of the car. Then they all stood around, kicking the ground with the toes of their sneakers, pounding Jordan on his upper arm, and trying not to cry. A lot of our neighbors came over to say goodbye, and Jordan hugged them all. By this time, Jordan was flat out sobbing. Ron put an arm around his shoulder. "Hey, man," he said, "there's no need for all that. You'll feel better once you start school and make some friends. You'll see. It's gonna be great."

Just before he got into the car, he turned to me and saw I had tears running down my cheeks. I held out my arms. Jordan stepped into them. He wrapped me in a long, silent squeeze, and then he was gone.

He didn't speak to me for four months after he moved to Florida. I'd call Ron to ask how he was doing, and even though the news was good—he was making friends and getting involved in activities at his new school—when Ron would yell for Jordan to come to the phone, he refused. I was devastated, but I didn't push. He was hurting as much as I was. Maybe more.

Again and again I replayed in my mind the evening I'd told Jordan that he would be moving to Jacksonville. "Mom, no, no, please! I'll behave! I don't want to live in Jacksonville. I want to stay here. My friends are here; my life is here. I'm not going to have the same kind of life down there that I have here."

"Jordan, you've got to go. It's time for your dad. It's time."

Jordan sank into a chair, and buried his face in his hands.

"Mom, you promised me."

I realized how the situation must look to him: I had gotten married and then two years later, I had sent him away. He felt as if I didn't want him anymore, as if he got in the way of my relationship with my new husband. Of course, nothing could have been further from the truth. For fifteen years, we had been a team, and now I wasn't sure he would ever forgive me.

Then one day when Ron called out to him, he came to the phone as if nothing had ever gone wrong between us. He began talking about the friends he'd made, and confided that even though he was new to the school, he'd captured the attention of some of the prettiest girls on the cheerleading squad. "Mom, you know I got game," he joked. I laughed at his conceit and asked him to tell me more. The long freeze had begun to thaw. Jordan and I would be close again. I had been absolved.

CHAPTER 10

Premonition

LATER, I WOULD ASK MYSELF a thousand times: If I hadn't sent Jordan to Jacksonville, would he still be alive? Where would he be now? What would he be doing? What kind of man would he be? There is no way to know.

After a rocky start at Samuel Wolfson High, Jordan pulled up his bootstraps and began applying himself to his studies. The other kids, attracted by his natural confidence, infectious laugh, and big-city swagger, called him "fresh" and flocked to him. Just as in Atlanta, Jordan was always at the center of a cluster of friends hanging out after school at his house.

Toward the end of Jordan's sophomore year, on an afternoon when he was scheduled to go to math tutoring, he and a friend decided to stop at the corner store for snacks. What they didn't know was that as they were heading through the alley to the shop, two men were holding up the cashier at gunpoint. They stole money from the till and then ran into the alley, where they confronted the two boys, demanding their wallets. The boys handed them over quickly and the gunmen continued down the alley and disappeared.

I was in West Palm Beach on a layover when Jordan called with this news. "Mom, I saw my life flash right before my eyes," he told me. "I was scared to death. I honestly thought I was going to die by a bullet today, and for a wallet with nothing in it."

I was so shaken that for almost an hour I wouldn't let Jordan off the phone. I was irrationally convinced that when we hung up, I would lose him. "Don't worry, Mom," Jordan assured me. "This experience showed me one thing: I will never own a gun. I don't like guns. I will never be around anybody who has them."

Still, I was concerned. Jordan definitely noticed differences between Jacksonville and Atlanta. Soon after he moved, he'd said to me: "Mom, I can feel this cloud over the city, like it's the seventies or something, like time just stopped. It's as if some people here don't know yet that black people are free. And the kids at school, they're really cool kids; you'd like them, Mom. But they don't have the same kinds of opportunities that we take for granted in Atlanta. They don't even have computers in their classes like we have."

To be honest, if I had truly understood how racially polarized that part of the state still was, how infused with the lingering attitudes of Jim Crow, I might have thought twice about sending Jordan to live there. I comforted myself that, living with Ron, he was surrounded by a loving, supportive community, and under his father's watchful care.

Now, however, he'd been held up at gunpoint several blocks from his school, something I could not have imagined happening to him. Of course, I was well aware that when people see few opportunities for their future, crime can take root, and on its heels, guns flow into the neighborhood. This is true in any disadvantaged community. That's why it always perplexes me when people make so much noise about so-called black-on-black crime. Whenever social advocates pursue ways to stop the flood of firearms into poor African American neighborhoods, or to address the senseless tragedy of hate crimes, or to confront a rise in gang activity, too often the stock response is: *You people are killing each other anyway. We can't (won't) address any of this until you deal with black-on-black crime.*

In fact, it's not that simple, because just as poverty has no color, crime has no color. It is strictly a socioeconomic phenomenon, with poor urban blacks committing violent crimes at statistically the same rate as poor urban whites—51.3 per 1,000 people for blacks compared to 56.4 per 1,000 for whites.[1] All this to say, black-on-black crime is a smokescreen meant to cloud the ways in which structural racism contributes to the persistence of inner cities plagued by poverty, poor schools, and bleak prospects. Viewed through this prism, the quickness of some to hide behind the excuse of black-on-black crime can be seen as just one more manifestation of a pervasive anti-black bias in American life.

———

America's anti-black bias would be on full display less than a year later. Jordan turned seventeen on February 16, 2012. Ten days later, a boy his age by the name of Trayvon Martin was shot and killed in Sanford, Florida, by a self-appointed neighborhood vigilante who thought the skinny black youth looked suspicious. Sanford was roughly a hundred miles south of Jacksonville. During halftime of the NBA All-Star Game, Trayvon had run out to get a pack of Skittles and a can of AriZona Iced Tea. On the way home, he pulled his gray hoodie up over his head to protect against the light rain. Meanwhile, George Zimmerman was tooling around the neighborhood in his SUV, on the lookout for trouble. Almost everyone in America has heard some version of what happened next.

When the 911 tapes of that evening were released several days later,

I made myself listen to them. In some part of me, I thought if I could understand how things had gone so horribly wrong for this child, I would know how to safeguard Jordan. Numerous calls from neighbors in the gated Sanford community had poured in to the police operator, all reporting a young man yelling for help. On one of the calls, I could hear Trayvon screaming, "Help me!" a total of fourteen times in the span of thirty-eight seconds. On another call, the cries for help were abruptly punctuated by a single gunshot. Then chilling silence, into which the man who made the call moaned, "Oh my God, oh my God, he's dead."

The first of the 911 calls had been from Zimmerman himself. He told police, "This guy looks like he's up to no good, or he's on drugs or something. He's just staring, looking at all the houses. Now he's coming toward me. He's got his hand in his waistband. Something's wrong with him." The operator told Zimmerman not to go after the young man, to wait for a police cruiser, but Zimmerman chased the teen down anyway. Trayvon called his girlfriend and told her that a strange man was following him, he didn't know why. She told him to run. He said he didn't want to, although eventually, he did. No doubt he knew that a young black man running is instantly taken for a suspect. But Trayvon was no criminal. He had no record. George Zimmerman, on the other hand, had numerous past violations. Yet when the police arrived and found Trayvon lifeless on the sidewalk's grassy verge, and Zimmerman holding a discharged firearm, they let the shooter go. They didn't even take his gun.

Zimmerman had claimed self-defense and invoked Florida's Stand Your Ground law. In such cases, if there is no one around to refute the shooter's claim of being threatened, he usually walks free. As all of America would soon learn, this is especially true if the victim is a black boy or man.

In the weeks that followed, many people were asking the same question: If the boy who was shot had been white, would the police have let Zimmerman go without filing any charges? But very few people were asking this: If the boy had been white, would the neighborhood watch captain even have noticed him walking home from the store? Everyone already knew the answer to that question. It was Danroy Henry, Sean Bell, Oscar Grant, and Amadou Diallo all over again in the sense that, in the "fast trap" of American consciousness, a black male was seen first and foremost as a suspect—guilty of *something*.

Michael Skolnik, a white writer for the online pop culture website Global Grind, made much the same observation:

> I will never look suspicious to you. Even if I have a black hoodie, a pair of jeans and white sneakers on . . . in fact, that is what I wore yesterday . . . I still will never look suspicious. No matter how much the hoodie covers my face or how baggie my jeans are, I will never look out of place to you. I will never watch a taxicab pass me by to pick someone else up. I will never witness someone clutch their purse tightly against their body as they walk by me. I won't have to worry about a police car following me for two miles, so they can run my plates. I will never have to pay before I eat. And I certainly will never get "stopped and frisked." I will never look suspicious to you, because of one thing and one thing only. The color of my skin . . .
>
> But, let's be clear. Let's be very, very clear. Before the neighborhood watch captain, George Zimmerman, started following [Trayvon Martin] against the better judgment of the 911 dispatcher. Before any altercation. Before any self-defense claim. Before Trayvon's cries for help were heard on the 911 tapes. Before the bullet hit him dead in the chest. Before all of this. He was suspicious. He was suspicious. Suspicious. And you know, like I know, it wasn't because of the hoodie or the jeans or the sneakers. Cause I had on that same

outfit yesterday and no one called 911 saying I was just wandering around their neighborhood. It was because of one thing and one thing only. Trayvon is black.[2]

Every time I thought about what happened to Trayvon, I ached for his parents, Sybrina Fulton and Tracy Martin. I couldn't conceive how they were coping, and yet they had graced the stages at protest marches across the country, stoic and dignified, calling on Americans to acknowledge a truth so basic it shouldn't even need to be proclaimed: black lives matter. African Americans and people of conscience took up the call. Marchers in cities across the country chanted Trayvon's name and wore hoodies in remembrance of an innocent young man with candy in his pocket walking home in the rain. They demanded that Florida's criminal justice system arrest Trayvon's killer for murder.

In quieter moments, black parents everywhere were reeling. We knew how to prepare our boys for confrontations with police officers carrying regulation firearms, but what were we to tell our children about a civilian with a gun in his hand and a stereotype in his head?

One night on a call-in news program, someone argued that if Trayvon had been afraid of Zimmerman, he should have just dialed 911. I was alone at home when I heard the comment, and all I could do was shake my head. The caller's statement plumbed the depths of what was not understood outside of black America—that a black boy *doesn't* call the police, because when the cops arrive, the person with black skin will be the first suspect they see. He'll be the one on whom they train their guns.

———

Jordan leaned against the windowsill in my bedroom, waiting for me as I searched in my closet for a sweater to put over my shoulders in church later that morning. A pale watercolor sun brushed the window-pane, outlining Jordan in light. He was visiting me in Atlanta for Easter weekend, and we were on our way to Sunday morning services at Trinity. I had no idea this would be my last Easter with my son, or that I would have only eight more months to be with him in physical form. The television was still on, tuned to a news station, and commentators were discussing Trayvon Martin. It was going on six weeks since law enforcement in Florida had declined to press charges against his killer.

"Mom, why did that man shoot Trayvon down?" Jordan asked me that morning. "Trayvon wasn't doing anything but walking home."

"I know, sweetie, I know."

I picked up my Bible and hymnal and turned to go. Curtis was already downstairs waiting for us in the car. But Jordan wasn't finished.

"I mean, why are they just gunning us down like animals?" he persisted.

I paused in the doorway and turned back to face my son, who hadn't moved from the window.

"Baby," I reminded him, "some people in this country will look at you and see only your skin color. They will not see *you*. They will not value your life. They won't recognize what is special and beloved about you. That's why I need you to always be vigilant about where you go, who you talk to, what you do. A lot of people out here don't have reasonable conflict-resolution skills. If they're upset with you, they're not going to try to talk it out. They'll just take out a gun and shoot you."

Even though I had often cautioned Jordan in this way, on that Sunday, he wasn't really hearing me.

"That's not going to happen to me," he declared, pounding his chest in a surge of sixteen-year-old bravado. "I can outrun a gun. I can wrestle the gun."

"Jordan, this is serious. You've got to watch yourself."

He shrugged, still focused on Trayvon, and the complete lack of reason behind his slaying. "I just don't understand how the law allowed that man to do what he did," he said. "What is wrong with the state of Florida?"

"Baby," I said, "this isn't only happening in Florida. This is happening all around the country. You have to be careful wherever you are."

"Oh, don't worry about me," he said, teen boy bravado welling up in him again. "I can take care of myself."

———

During that last summer of his life, Jordan spent several weekends back in Marietta with Curtis and me, sometimes staying into the week. The adolescent bluster I'd noticed in him over Easter break was on less visible display. In its place was a new thoughtfulness, almost a brooding aspect. Night after night as I prepared dinner for the family, Jordan would settle himself at the kitchen table to talk. Our conversations were deep reflections about God and faith, the purpose of human suffering, heaven and the afterlife. We also talked about America's original sin—the racial subjugation of black people to justify the inhumanity of slavery, and the nation's continued oppression through such caste systems as Jim Crow and the unequal treatment of black and brown people in the criminal justice system.

Eventually, the talk would turn again to Trayvon Martin. The special prosecutor appointed to the case, Angela Corey, had reconsidered letting Zimmerman walk free. Two months after the fact, she had brought charges of second-degree murder against Trayvon's killer, who was now in custody. Amid wall-to-wall news coverage of the case, Jordan made some piercing observations.

"Why wasn't Trayvon Martin the one to stand *his* ground?" he asked me one evening as I was chopping onions for a stew. "Wasn't he the one being chased? Wasn't he the one in danger?"

I realized my son had been studying the details of the case. And he was absolutely right—there was something fundamentally wrong with a law that allowed a person to claim self-defense even though he was the pursuer. Zimmerman had gone after this child despite explicit instruction from the 911 dispatcher not to do so. On the 911 tapes, in the moment he decided to ignore the police, Zimmerman could be heard muttering, "These assholes always get away." Clearly, the only one threatened that night was Trayvon Martin, who so many people heard screaming for help before a gunshot silenced him.

"It's a good point," I told Jordan, "but I think we both know the answer."

Inevitably, Jordan would circle back to the same question. "Mom, what will you do when I die?"

"Jordan, why do you keep asking me that?" I said, exasperated.

"'Cause I need to know, Mom. I need to know if you're going to be okay when I'm gone."

Much later, I would remember Jordan saying *when* and not *if*. I would wonder why I had paid so little attention to his choice of words.

"Oh, son, you're not going to die," I insisted. "You're going to do great things."

This usually provoked a laugh from Jordan. "Yes!" he would declare playfully. "Everybody is going to know *my* name!"

Jordan and I must have had that identical conversation a hundred times that summer. Once, perplexed by the fact that he seemed to be so intently contemplating the possibility of his own death, I said seriously, "You know, son, if anything were to happen to you, that would be like me dying, too. And yet I'd be forced to move forward because God commands that. I imagine if God called you home, God would take care of me, too."

We were quiet for a while, considering this. But I couldn't abide the somberness of the moment for long, so I lightened the mood by punching his arm gently and saying, "But nothing's going to happen to you, Jordan. Now you stop talking like that!"

Maybe it was the frequency of these conversations, or perhaps it was God whispering to me, but for some not-quite-understood reason, I felt compelled to fly Jordan to visit our relatives all over the country that summer. We traveled from Chicago to San Diego to New York, spending time with Jordan's aunts and uncles and cousins. "Your family needs to see you," I told him each time I proposed another trip. "They need to spend time with you." Jordan never resisted or complained. In retrospect, he made a singular effort to connect with each family member. I remember being surprised and moved by the intentional ways in which he expressed his care for every one of them. One evening in San Diego, for example, when Jordan and his aunt Lori were at the house alone, Jordan said to her out of the blue, "Aunt Lori, I want to thank you for praying for me. God has shown me how much you pray for me, and I want you to know, I'm going to be okay."

At the time Lori had found his comment strange, because even though she did indeed ask God daily to care for her nephew, she had never mentioned this to him. Moved by the sincere feeling in his words, she had wrapped Jordan in her arms, put her cheek against his, and rocked him side to side. When Lori told me later what Jordan had said, it reminded me of a night when he had asked, yet again, if I would be able to move on if he died. We were in my car, headed to the airport so he could board a flight back to Jacksonville after spending the week with me. I pulled into the terminal parking lot, turned off the ignition, and turned to face my son. "Jordan," I said, "I believe that you're going to live a long, fruitful life. You're going to go on to college or join the Marines, and you're going to get married and give me grandbabies. God has promised me that."

Jordan shook his head. "No, Mom, no," he said with some urgency. "You *don't* know what God has in store for me. You have no idea what God has in store for us."

We were both silent in the dark car, then Jordan said, "But I know one thing: when my time comes, I'll be ready to go, because I know where I'm going. I'll be with Jesus and my unborn brother Lucien, and you all will be the ones here on earth trying to ease people's suffering."

He sounded so matter-of-fact that I hadn't known how to respond. I simply said, "Come on, son, get your things. You don't want to miss the flight."

But his words haunted me. I wanted to think I knew what was ahead for us, but did I really? From the time Jordan was little, I had prayed to God to use him for an extraordinary purpose, that he might leave his mark on the world. I had invented all sorts of wonderful futures for him, always involving good works in the material world. Not in a million years did I suspect what God's will for Jordan might be.

Later, we would all wonder whether Jordan had been having premonitions. Ron recalled a night in Jacksonville when he looked out from the kitchen and saw our boy sitting in his favorite chair on the back patio. Jordan could sit there for hours, lulled by the sound of a rocky waterfall flowing into the lake at the far end of the lawn. On this night, Ron went out to join his son, two glasses of lemonade in his hands. As he held out one glass to Jordan, he saw that his face was soaked with tears.

"Son, what's wrong?" he said, alarmed.

To this day, Ron cannot make sense of Jordan's answer.

"Dad, I don't think I'm meant to make it."

CHAPTER 11

Ten Bullets

WITH MY SON NO LONGER in my everyday care, I felt a little lost—classic empty nest syndrome. For sixteen years I had been completely focused on raising Jordan, and now I needed something new in my life to fill the hours I had previously devoted to him. I'd always loved the theater, and so I enrolled in acting classes. Soon I was auditioning for roles on stage, on camera, and in television commercials. I managed to get cast in several commercials and even a couple of movies. One of the films was called *Stand Your Ground*. I played Mrs. Reymundo, a middle-aged Latina mother who lost her son to gun violence under the Stand Your Ground law. Seriously. You can look it up. There I was, filming that role in February 2012, with not a clue that before the end of the year, I would suffer the very anguish I was imitating for the sake of art. Was God trying to prepare me for what was to come? The Lord certainly works in mysterious ways.

That fall, Jordan told me he had a girlfriend. Her name was Aliyah and she was new to his class and a cheerleader. She and Jordan had become Wolfson High's de facto power couple, two physically beautiful young people with a glow on them. Aliyah did well in her studies, worked three jobs, and was definitely going places. She convinced Jordan to hit the books harder and get his head in the game for whatever came after graduation. Ron and I loved the influence she was having on our boy. Then he and Aliyah had a fuss. The way I understood it, Jordan had bought red roses for her birthday, but refused to give them to her at school because he didn't want the other kids to tease him. Aliyah thought his excuse was lame, and she turned cool toward my boy. Jordan was determined to get back in her good graces. He confessed to me that he'd never liked anyone the way he liked Aliyah, with her mane of wavy dark hair and clear brown eyes, and the fact that she didn't stand for any foolishness.

When we talked on Thanksgiving morning, Jordan told me he wanted to find just the right Christmas present for his girl. Over the phone, we discussed gift ideas. Jewelry or a fashion accessory of some sort, I'd suggested, or maybe sneakers in a hot style. Jordan himself was a bit of a sneaker head. Picturing him stepping out in his favorite red Vans always made me smile. I wished again that Jordan had traveled to Chicago with us. The day before Curtis and I left, he'd called to say he wanted to join us for Thanksgiving in Atlanta. I explained that we'd already committed to spending the holiday with his aunt Terry and uncle Earl up north, and urged him to come with us. "Nah," he said. "I'll just stay here with Dad."

He thought maybe he'd go shopping for Black Friday deals with his friends. They had talked about cruising the Town Center mall, hoping to run into some cute girls they knew. Jordan didn't plan to do much cruising. Instead, he would stop by Urban Outfitters, where Aliyah worked, to smooth things over with his girl.

Tommie Stornes was at the wheel of his red Dodge Durango. He was nineteen years old, with a lean, chiseled face framed by dreadlocks. He'd already finished high school and was figuring out what was next for him. The other boys in the car, Tevin Thompson, Leland Brunson, and Jordan were all seventeen, due to graduate the following June. Jordan had talked about joining the Marines like his older cousin Julian had done. Leland, slight of frame with a thin, earnest face, was planning to go to college. He was Jordan's best friend in Jacksonville, a soft-spoken young man who was in the same grade as Jordan at Wolfson High. Tevin was the jovial one, tall and robustly built with a genial smile. He was a twelfth grader at Atlantic Coast High School across town, and he and Tommie sometimes teamed up to make rap music videos with their friends. They were good boys being raised with strong values in solid middle-class homes. Ron knew them all. He was used to cooking up waffles for them as they played video games in his living room, and he didn't have a moment's hesitation about Jordan spending the day with these well-mannered young men.

On toward evening, Jordan met up with Aliyah. The two of them spent a little while talking and laughing inside the store, and by the time Jordan left with his friends, everything was good again. In fact, Aliyah had wanted him to stay longer and go shopping with her, but the other boys were ready to leave. Aliyah told Jordan she'd call later that night when her shift was over, and they could talk some more. My son was in high spirits as he and his friends piled into the car. They discussed whether to head home or hit another mall across town.

They decided to head to another shopping center, but first Tommie wanted to pick up a pack of Newports and some gum. If they were going to be on the lookout for girls, they had to have fresh breath. As they pulled out of the Town Center mall parking lot and into heavy Black Friday traffic, Tevin leaned forward, tuning the car stereo, looking for his station. A thumping hip-hop baseline filled the car. When I imagine the boys in this moment, they are happy, bopping their heads, snapping their fingers, playing imaginary drums in the air.

At the intersection of Baymeadows Road and Southside Boulevard, Tommie turned into the Gate Gas Station and parked in front of the convenience store. Rap music blared from the stereo as he opened his door. He was dancing to the beat as he disappeared into the minimart. Moments later, a black Jetta pulled into the parking spot on Tevin and Jordan's side. The driver parked so close to Tommie's car that if Tevin or Jordan had wanted to open their doors all the way, they would not have been able to. There were several empty spots on either side of them, but the broad-chested white man at the wheel of the Jetta chose the slot right next to the car in which three young black men were listening to rap music. The boys didn't pay him any mind at first. They hardly noticed as a brown-haired woman in heels exited the Jetta on the far side and followed Tommie into the store.

It was just past 7:30 PM, and the song "Beef" by rapper Lil Reese was playing. The man in the next car rolled down his window and called: "Turn that music down. I can't hear myself think." His tone conveyed his annoyance.

I have no doubt, given what I have since learned about Michael Dunn, that he looked over at Tommie's SUV and saw not three teenagers innocently vibing to the beat, but a car full of hoodlums playing what he called "thug music." As Tevin would later observe, for men like Dunn, "*Thug* is the new *N-word*. That's the new way they're pursuing us now. *N-word* is out and *thug* is in." Tevin continued: "Michael Dunn, he just saw four black kids and he heard the music and he just instantly put the word *thug* next to us. But if four white kids were listening to it, what would you think? It's like they don't call Justin Bieber a thug . . . He's just a misled kid."[1]

Certainly something in the man's tone rubbed Jordan the wrong way, because as Tevin started to turn down the dial, Jordan reached over the car seat and stopped him. "Fuck that," he said. "Turn the music back up." And Tevin did, though not as loud.

Jordan and the man in the Jetta began arguing. A shopper walking back to his car from the convenience store heard someone shout: "You're not gonna talk to me like that!" The voice was so loud and so angry that he turned to see who was yelling. He noticed a white man in a black Jetta reach for something inside his car, and then he saw the glint of a pistol. By then Tommie had returned and was fastening his seat belt. Tevin had turned down the music to explain to Tommie what was happening. That's when Tommie saw the gun outside Tevin's window. "Duck!" he screamed as he slammed the car into reverse. A bullet whizzed by his head, clipping the visor. He heard the *ping ping ping* of gunshots piercing the outer shell of his car, and the sound of glass shattering. Witnesses said that as Tommie backed away, Dunn exited his Jetta and crouched beside it, still firing. Tommie floored the gas pedal and sped forward until he couldn't see the man with the gun anymore, or hear his volleys popping off like firecrackers. Only when he was safely in the lot of an adjacent shopping plaza did he come to a screeching halt.

He jumped out and circled his car to survey the damage and check on his boys. He called their names one by one, but only two of his friends answered. The window next to where Tevin was sitting was shot through, and the door below it was pocked by three holes, but the steel ate the bullets, and Tevin was unhurt. In the back seat, Leland, too, had escaped injury, but on the passenger side, three shots had drilled all the way through, lodging themselves in Jordan's body. My son had collapsed sideways, falling against Leland, whose hands, trying to pull him to safety, came away sticky and red.

Leland cradled his best friend and sobbed.

"He's not moving," he cried. "He's not moving."

Tevin got out of the front seat and pulled open the back door of the Durango, yelling Jordan's name. "Jordan was making that rattle people make when they're dying," he later recalled.[2] Then Tevin saw the black Jetta moving toward the exit of the Gate Gas Station. Panicked that the shooting would start up again he quickly slammed the back door and got back in the front passenger seat. Tommie, too, jumped back in the car and restarted the engine. All he could think to do was head to the brightest spot nearby to get help. He drove back to the Gate Gas Station while Tevin called 911.

The entire confrontation, from the time Dunn pulled up to the convenience store to the moment when Tommie brought the car to a stop in the adjacent shopping plaza, had lasted three-and-a-half minutes. That's how long it took for a white man with a gun to become incensed enough to spray bullets into a car holding four unarmed black teenagers.

———

The parking lot was strobed by flashing lights. Wailing sirens split the night as detectives rounded up and interviewed dozens of witnesses and took statements from the three boys. Next to the Durango, paramedics worked furiously on Jordan, who had been pulled out of the back seat and laid out on the ground. Their efforts were in vain. Our child was pronounced dead upon arrival at Shands Hospital. Much later that night, when detectives told Ron what had provoked the shooting, he shook his head in disbelief. "You mean my son is dead because somebody thought his *music* was too loud?"

The shooter had long departed the scene. Witnesses saw him get back into his car as his fiancée ran out of the store. He and his fiancée drove back to the hotel where they were staying overnight, and never called the police. Nor did they call any of the family members with whom they'd spent the afternoon at the wedding of Dunn's son. They had left the reception early to go back to their hotel to check on their dog, stopping at the convenience store on the way so Rouer could pick up a bottle of wine and some chips. When the shooting started, she had rushed out of the store, leaving her purchases next to the cash register. The next morning, after seeing news reports that one of the boys Dunn fired on had been killed, they drove nearly three hours south to Satellite Beach, Florida, where Dunn lived in an oceanfront condo.

Fortuitously, a young homeless man named Shawn Atkins had jotted down the black Jetta's license plate number on a store receipt, which is how law enforcement knew where to find my son's killer. Police arrived at noon the next day to question him. At six-foot-four and almost three hundred pounds, Michael Dunn was an imposing figure, dressed in a light-colored, short-sleeved bush jacket and plaid shorts. He greeted the police officers quizzically, as if he had no clue why they were standing at his door. Police detectives took him down to the precinct house where he reportedly waived his Miranda rights and declined to call a lawyer.

During interrogation, Dunn claimed that he had shot at the four African American teens in self-defense. He appeared convinced that he had done nothing wrong. Did he truly think he would simply walk away? I don't pretend to know his mind-set beyond the fact that he had looked at Jordan and saw not my cherished child, but a disposable being on whom he could vent his rage that a black boy would dare to talk back to him, to defy his command to turn the music down.

It was only after police formally arrested Dunn and charged him with first-degree murder and three counts of attempted murder that he hired a lawyer, Robin Lemonidis. At this point, Dunn's story about the boys threatening him with a weapon became his main defense.

Lemonidis told reporters that the four boys had pointed a gun, or maybe it was a metal pipe, Dunn wasn't sure, but they pointed *something* at him. "All he sees are heavily tinted windows, which are up, and the back windows, which are down, and the car has at least four black men in it," Lemonidis said. "And he doesn't know how old anybody is, he doesn't know anything, but he knows a shotgun when he sees one."

Through his lawyer, Dunn described the four teenagers as if they were hardened gangbangers about to call their thug friends for backup. He had to stop them before their friends arrived, he said. And that was why he had feared for his life—and why he was invoking the cover of Stand Your Ground.

As soon as Lemonidis made Stand Your Ground the centerpiece of Michael Dunn's defense, Ron and I realized that he meant to use the "scary black man" argument as his justification for committing murder. Worse, it was possible that white southern jurors, steeped in the same racial soup as the defendant, just might sympathize with his story. It became crystal clear that getting justice for Jordan was not going to be easy. We had a fight on our hands.

—————

The idea behind Stand Your Ground can be traced all the way back to English common law, the foundation of which was the sanctity of human life. In England in the 1600s, the only person permitted to end a life was the king. All other citizens had an obligation to retreat to "the wall behind your back" in the event of a conflict, and only then would it be considered reasonable to fight back against an attacker using deadly force. If, however, there remained any possibility of retreat, all parties had a duty to deescalate the situation and avoid the loss of life. The only exception to this rule of law pertained to one's home: if a man was attacked within the confines of his living quarters, he was allowed to defend the sanctity of his house. In this circumstance, the individual was not required to retreat before meeting the situation with deadly force. The underlying idea was that "the house of every one is to him as his castle and fortress, as well as for his defence against injury and violence, as for his repose."[3] The law became known as the castle doctrine.

In practice, the castle doctrine didn't cover everyone. Back in the seventeenth century, the law effectively protected only white, moneyed, property-owning Englishmen. A woman could not invoke the castle doctrine against, for example, an abusive husband, nor could the colonized, the poor, the indentured, or the enslaved successfully "stand their ground" against white men of the propertied class. In the United States, whose constitution was based on English common law, this state of affairs also held true.

Caroline Light, a professor of gender studies at Harvard University and author of *Stand Your Ground: A History of America's Love Affair with Lethal Self-Defense*, asserts that there is an "alchemy of different power structures that conspired to turn the United States into a place that celebrated a particular kind of heroic, white, frontier ruggedness, and capacity to spread from sea to shining sea through manifest destiny."[4] As Light further explains, those in power tend to act in ways that will reinforce that power, and that includes how the castle doctrine has come to be applied in self-defense firearm cases. "Our long history of self-defensive lethal violence is steeped in a certain kind of structure of power that tends to concentrate power in the hands of those who already have it," she reflects.[5]

In the newly birthed nation of America, as in seventeenth-century England, those already in possession of power were white men of property and means. Others—women, people of color, the poor, the indentured and enslaved—seldom, if ever, experienced the laws of the country applied for their protection. Only the power elite could be sure of the shelter of the fledgling nation's legal system. Indeed, the Second Amendment—which states in full that "a well regulated Militia, being necessary to the security of a free State, the right of the people to keep and bear Arms, shall not be infringed"—was crafted for the express purpose of guarding the framers of those words, the white male elite, against incursions on their power from any quarter.

In latter years, the National Rifle Association and the firearm industry have sought to expand the power class of gun owners who worship at the altar of the Second Amendment. They have achieved this in part by agitating to pass laws that transform the duty to retreat into an inalienable right to defend one's castle—now redefined to include one's physical person—against any perceived threat. The new law, first adopted in Florida in 2005, was called Stand Your Ground. In the run-up to its successful passage in the state legislature, the NRA aggressively instructed its members about lethal self-defense under the law—and under God. They insisted that gun owners had not just the right, but also a divine responsibility to protect their castles against intrusion. And that castle now traveled with them, effectively encompassing wherever they legally stood.

What made this promotion of deadly self-defense so dangerous to communities of color was the gun lobby's broad characterization of them as menacing. Urban black and brown people were cast in the pro-gun narrative as moral miscreants, hardened criminals, thugs, and animals, an ever-present threat to white America's safety and survival. It was a tried and true dog whistle, subversively delivered through overhyped stories on NRATV and in the organization's print and online media. All of it was expressly designed to stoke ancient hostilities in white nationalists opposed to the so-called browning of America, and righteous fervor in the political entity known as the Christian Right, people who, while not always religious, were nevertheless convinced they had the Word of God on their side. These mostly rural conservatives were persuaded to stockpile guns in a bid to protect and preserve their God-given freedoms.

Perhaps equally as seductive as the call to take up arms was that the gun lobby's narrative also served to elevate poor whites above historically subjugated groups, offering them a common context with the propertied class, the rich white men who make and apply the laws. Not surprisingly, Stand Your Ground would only serve to intensify the divisive racial dynamic around guns, putting the nation's most vulnerable and historically disenfranchised citizens at the greatest risk. It was at this deadly crossroads of guns and race that my son would lose his life.

CHAPTER 12

The Right to Exist

WE WILL ALWAYS LOVE YOU, *Jordan*.

One of Jordan's classmates at Wolfson High shyly walked up to me at his memorial service. He held out a sheaf of yellow notepaper on which Jordan's classmates had composed messages to him. "I'm so sorry, Mrs. Davis," he mumbled, his eyes downcast. I took the squares of yellow paper and thanked him, and then impulsively I pulled him to me and hugged him. It meant so much to know that Jordan had been loved in the place where he had died. In the months to come, I would take out that little stack of yellow paper and read again and again the words his friends had written:

You were an amazing guy with such a great personality.

I still remember when you would run up and hug me.

I will never forget all the times you would make me laugh.

And this one, perhaps my favorite:

Oh my God, I can't believe you're gone. I love and miss you so much. I was looking forward to doing music with you but now I know that will be in another life.

Perhaps those words resonated so deeply with me because I felt as if I had been slammed into another life entirely. Who was I now, if not Jordan Davis's mother? From the first moment I had held my newborn to my heart, being Jordan's mother had been my primary role, my utter commitment. Now, I felt adrift, anchored to nothing at all, the ground falling soundlessly away. For weeks after Jordan died, I did not feel as if I was even on this earth.

I went through the motions, showing up at my son's memorial service at Giddens Funeral Home in Jacksonville. Standing beside my son's casket, I placed my palm over the Bible tucked beneath his hand. And I prayed: *Lord, please carry me now. I need you more than ever before. Thank you for giving Jordan to me for seventeen precious years. Mothering him has been the best thing I have ever done. What a blessing and honor it has been to be his mother. Take good care of him, Lord. And show me what I am to do now. Show me why you have taken my child from me. I don't want his death to be in vain.*

For a long time, I stood there and listened hard for God's still, small voice inside me. But I heard only silence. I felt a rush of anger: *Why Jordan, Lord? What did we ever do to deserve this sorrow?*

I had tried so hard to raise my son to love and please the Lord. This was not the reward I had imagined. I felt bereft of faith and poor in understanding, and for the first time in my life, I railed at God. Sensing my anger and turmoil, Curtis moved to my side, circled my shoulders with one arm, and led me back to my seat. My vision blurred by tears, I leaned into him gratefully. He was there for me in every way possible, and yet I had never felt more alone.

Back at Ron's condo, we finalized plans to fly Jordan's body home to Atlanta the next morning. We would hold a viewing for family and friends at Cobb Funeral Home in Marietta that evening, and then lay our beautiful boy to rest during an 11 AM memorial service at Trinity Chapel on Friday.

After all the preparations had been made, Ron, Carolina, Curtis, and I collapsed in the living room, still in our mourning clothes, wrung out from the emotion of the day. In that lull, Ron's cell phone pinged with a message from Tracy Martin, the father of Trayvon, a man whose naked grief we had witnessed from a distance on the nightly news. "I just want to welcome you to a club that no one wants to belong to," Tracy wrote. He added that if ever we needed anything, we had only to call him or Trayvon's mother, Sybrina. They both knew intimately what we were going through.

Tracy's text message was on my mind as we boarded the Delta flight home to Atlanta on Thursday morning. Acutely aware of my son's body in a long white box in the cargo hold below us, I was barely holding it together. But Tracy's words reminded me that countless parents before me had weathered this exact pain, and many of them had transformed their suffering into action. Tracy and Sybrina were helping to birth the Black Lives Matter movement, just as fifty-seven years before, another senseless death, Emmett Till's, had led his mother to help launch the civil rights movement. I understood their burden now, the agony of knowing that if my child had been born white, he might still be alive. And yet, I didn't dare crumble in the face of this sorrow. I needed to stand firm and bear the great weight of it, as others had borne it, because we had work to do. We had to help create a world in which no other parent would have to join our brokenhearted club.

Delta Airlines had seated Ron, Carolina, Curtis, and me in first class, and the flight crew could not have been more solicitous. The child of Delta employees, Jordan was one of their own. As we pulled away from the tarmac and taxied down the runway, the pilot's voice came over the sound system. "As a memorial to our employees' fallen son who is traveling home with us today, we will be spraying the plane on takeoff and landing," he told the passengers. Immediately, jets of water washed over the aircraft from both sides. It was a salute usually reserved for pilots on their last flight before retirement, or for casualties of war whose bodies were being returned to their families. Watering the plane was the crew's way of saying farewell to someone esteemed; the spray represented symbolic tears for the final journey of a hero. As I watched the water pour down the cabin's windows, my own tears flowed.

An hour and ten minutes after this moving tribute orchestrated by my colleagues, we pulled up to the gate in Atlanta, and the pilot asked the passengers to stay seated until we disembarked. Several of my fellow flight attendants met us in the terminal and escorted us down to the tarmac. There, Delta agents in full dress uniform stood in a solemn receiving line as our son's casket was removed from the cargo hold. All the ground crew we knew were there, all the people who worked on the ramp, all the gate agents, all our supervisors, they had all come to welcome Jordan home, to stand with us as his casket was placed on the special cart reserved for fallen soldiers. One of Ron's friends who worked in the baggage area had arranged everything, right down to a black town car that drove onto the tarmac to ferry us to the parking lot where we had left our car just days before. It seemed like a far distant lifetime.

The love surrounding Jordan's homecoming continued that evening. On the Internet, a grassroots effort to honor my son urged people across the nation to "turn the music up" at 6 PM, when his wake was scheduled to begin. The viewing was supposed to run until 8 PM, but at nine that night the line of mourners still stretched around the block. Hundreds of people waited patiently to pay their last respects to our son. It seemed everyone who had ever been part of our lives in Atlanta came out to see him. There were so many people it would have been impossible to receive them one by one that evening. In the end, Ron and I asked people to crowd into the chapel so that we could thank everyone at once. I spoke first. I expressed my gratitude that so many had come out to show their love and support. "This is what Jordan wanted," I told the crowd. "Jordan always said, 'When I die I want a huge party, and I want everybody I love to be there.' Well, Jordan, I know you didn't expect it to come this way but everybody who loves you, they're here."

———

News people had been camped outside of Ron's house since the morning after the shooting, and back in Marietta, a press vehicle was waiting outside our home as we pulled up. They filmed us going inside the house, but respected our request for no interviews. Other television news trucks cruised up and down our street, with some reporters knocking on doors to talk to our neighbors. At Jordan's funeral at Trinity Chapel on Friday morning, reporters attempted to question family and friends who were filing into the church. Eventually, a church administrator asked them to stand across the street and allow the mourners to say goodbye to Jordan in peace.

As disruptive as the news people could be, I was grateful that my son's life and death mattered to them, and that they wanted to tell our story. Journalists were often able to run down information about our case before we knew it ourselves. And it had been a local newscaster who connected us with our attorney in Jacksonville. The newswoman was a friend of Ron's, and the godmother of our lawyer's son. I had my doubts about John Phillips at first, but it didn't take me long to realize he was heaven-sent.

When I first met him in Ron's living room a few days after Jordan's death, I remember thinking that he seemed very young. I wondered how many cases he'd tried, and how experienced he was. And then there was the fact that he was white. Given the racial overtones of our case, I wondered whether we might need an African American lawyer, someone versed in the ways in which the shoot-first law endangered young black men. But as we sat and spoke with John that first evening, the feeling that came through stronger than all the others was that he had a heart. By the time he had finished exploring with us how we would have to confront Dunn's self-defense claim, there was no question in my mind or in Ron's: we wanted to move forward.

My husband, Curtis, was not of the same mind, however. He had seen what happened in numerous other cases of unarmed black men shot and killed by white men for no reason that made sense to him. Invariably, he said, after a long, drawn-out legal process, sometimes lasting for years, the victim was painted as a morally corrupt hoodlum, sometimes based on "facts" conjured out of thin air. Did we really want to drag Jordan's name through the mud like that, and then have his killer walk free? Our involvement would only lead to prolonged anguish for the family, Curtis argued, with no closure at the end. Curtis wanted us to leave the prosecuting of Michael Dunn to the Duval County State Attorney's Office, while we went back to Atlanta and picked up the pieces of our lives. "I'm just saying consider it," he said. "You need to heal from all this. We need to move on."

"Move *on?*" I said, my tone incredulous. I knew Curtis meant well, but I still couldn't believe what he was proposing. "Do you really think I can physically walk away from what was done to Jordan and not seek justice on his behalf? Do you think I won't be in that courtroom every single day? I know it's going to be hard, but Jordan would *expect* me to stand up for him. He would *expect* me to fight with my last breath, because that is what I was teaching him."

Curtis loved Jordan deeply, and I knew I had to give him space to mourn him in his own way, but I also needed him to understand that I was forever changed. To be perfectly candid, those months after we laid our boy to rest were rough on our marriage. Each of us was locked inside our own pain. Perhaps our very worst night was when Curtis said, "If only Jordan had just kept his mouth shut, he'd be alive today."

His words sliced right through me, and suddenly I was flying at him, shrieking and bawling and pounding my fists on his chest.

"How could you say that?" I screeched. "How could you say such a thing? Whether Jordan kept his mouth shut or not, he didn't deserve to die! It didn't matter how loud his music was! It doesn't matter what he said! He didn't deserve that man shooting him dead!"

Realizing too late how his comment had cut me, Curtis tried to catch my wheeling hands and fold me to him, but I pushed him roughly away. "No!" I yelled, blinded by rage and pain. "Don't you touch me!" And then I was crumpled on the floor, crying so hard I thought my heart would explode out of my chest. I forced myself up and ran to Jordan's room, throwing myself down on his bed. "Lord, I can't do this," I wailed. "I don't know if I can get through this."

For the next several nights I couldn't bring myself to sleep anywhere but in Jordan's bed, surrounded by the things he had loved, the favorite T-shirts his dad had returned to me, his well-used Xbox, the brown hoodie he grabbed every morning, the red sneakers he wore everywhere. I lay among his orphaned belongings, brooding on what Curtis had said. Perhaps the hardest part was knowing that Curtis would not be the only one to harbor such a thought. Again and again, I put myself inside Tommie Stornes's car on the night Jordan was killed. I couldn't deny that in the turbulence of my own grief, I, too, had often wished that Jordan had chosen not to verbally engage with Michael Dunn. And yet I understood why he had done it. I had not a shred of doubt that Jordan believed he was standing up for himself and for his friends.

I had raised my boy to understand that he was as good as anyone else. I wanted him to be proud as a black man. I had taught him to stand tall and look everyone in the eye. "Don't you ever let anyone demean you," I'd tell him. I said it so often that he'd roll his eyes as he answered, "Yes, Mom, I know, I know, you say this all the time." To which I'd respond, "Well, I just want to be sure you get it."

This was the context in which I understood Jordan's instinctive response to Michael Dunn. It wasn't about the music. For Jordan, it was about the way Dunn spoke to him and his boys. I'm certain Jordan perceived that to Dunn, he and his friends had no value. To him, they were worthless. When Jordan told Tevin to turn the music back up, what he was really doing was standing up for his boys. He was defending their right to exist—to hold space in the world alongside men like Dunn. He was saying, "You can't talk to us as if we're less than nothing and expect us to respect your request. We have as much right to be in this place as you do." In Jordan's eyes, they were four black teens raised by parents who'd taught them right from wrong. They weren't doing anything illegal. They were just having some innocent fun. And whatever people might feel about how Jordan conducted himself, no matter how we might wish to call back the F-bombs traded with an angry white man with a pistol in his car, there was no excuse for Michael Dunn to pump my child full of lead.

I sat down with Curtis a few days later, and tried to calmly explain why his comment about Jordan keeping his mouth shut had so gutted me. I pointed out that black boys in America are denied the right to be vulnerable, to make mistakes, to indulge in harmless adolescent bravado. Indeed, numerous studies have shown that black children of both genders are seen as less innocent, more culpable, than white children of the same age. Sadly, the real-world consequence can be the kind of violence that kills boys like Jordan, a high school senior who had never been in trouble with the law, but whom Michael Dunn insisted looked to him like a full-grown man, a shotgun-carrying gangbanger.

Now imagine for a moment that Jordan and his friends were a car full of unarmed white boys, playing music at the same loud volume, and a black man had argued with them, then shot into their car, killing one of them. The whole country would be up in arms. Not a single person would accept the claim of self-defense, nor would they ever consider justifying the shooting under Stand Your Ground. This reverse scenario makes it clear that gun laws weren't created to protect black people. Ever since the Second Amendment was crafted by the Founding Fathers, gun laws have been designed to be used against us, to justify white men like Michael Dunn profiling black males, shooting first, explaining later.

And yet, it is too simple to label what happened to Jordan as a hate crime. People like Michael Dunn, a gun collector since his youth, operate with a mind-set of historic entitlement encoded in the very laws of the land. I am convinced that, had there been no Stand Your Ground statute to provide him cover, Dunn might have thought twice before reaching for his handgun, and Jordan might still be alive. To protect others from the fate my son suffered, I would have to get involved in helping to dismantle this dangerous law. My education as a gun-violence-prevention advocate had begun.

CHAPTER 13

A Wider Lens

LAWRENCE O'DONNELL OF MSNBC CALLED. Through our attorney, he had invited Ron and me to fly to New York and appear on his nightly news program, *The Last Word*. John Phillips explained that O'Donnell wanted to talk with us about Stand Your Ground and how the law was complicating our efforts to get justice for our son. Less than three weeks had gone by since Jordan took his final breath, but, as raw as we were, Ron and I didn't hesitate. We knew we had to help inform others about the dangers of this gun law. Just as compelling was our desire to let the people know what had happened to our son. We wanted the world to understand who Jordan had been, and how much had been lost, not just by his family, but also by everyone whose life he might have touched as he fulfilled the great promise we saw in him.

We had to be judicious in how we presented our case, however. Ron and I were relieved that John Phillips was on the same page as we were when it came to protecting Jordan's image. He had seen how partisan observers on social media had pounced on Trayvon Martin's character, spinning a narrative of him as a young punk. A white supremacy group had actually hacked the teen's email and social media accounts, spreading misinformation and running photographs of Trayvon wearing a gold grill on his teeth. It was a moment of harmless posturing in the life of an adolescent boy, yet it was played as evidence to support the claim that the slight-of-frame seventeen-year-old, a boy who weighed at least fifty pounds less than his killer, had made Zimmerman fear for his life. To make matters worse, law enforcement took this dead child who had been *running away* from his killer, and who had nothing on his person but candy and a can of iced tea, and they tested his body for drugs. Yet they neglected to test the gun that was still smoking in Zimmerman's hand when they arrived. Instead they sent him home with it, squandering an opportunity to gather critical evidence.

To this day, I cannot wrap my mind around Trayvon being tested for drugs. Did they imagine that a positive result would explain a strange man pursuing him when all he was doing was walking home? Was that supposed to justify Zimmerman shooting him through the heart? Of course not—just as Jordan arguing with Dunn did not justify his murder. But in so many cases when an unarmed victim is black and the shooter white, the ensuing public narrative smears the victim's character with insinuations of criminality, as if to suggest the killing was warranted.

John Phillips had observed the shameful character assassination of Trayvon Martin. He wanted to help us make sure that the same would not happen to Jordan, especially given the similar racial dynamics in the two cases based on the shooters' self-defense claims. He assisted Ron and me as we carefully assessed each interview request, because, as John put it, "You're just exposing your soul every time. The media starts off like a little fish that has to eat the bigger fish, which has to eat the bigger fish. At some point that fish might get so big it turns and bites you."

It was true that the two cases were different in that the police had arrested, interrogated, and charged Michael Dunn with murder within a day. Trayvon's killer was not charged until more than a month after the shooting. It had taken a national outcry to get Florida law enforcement to take a second look at the case. As Benjamin Crump, the attorney for Trayvon's family, had pointed out, "Martin's parents had to be present in the media to say that authorities are not going to arrest the killer of their unarmed child. They were forced to do interviews to get simple justice."

Another major difference was that no one had seen Zimmerman shoot and kill Trayvon, whereas dozens of people had seen Michael Dunn crouched and firing off shot after shot at Tommie's wildly retreating car. Yet even with an arrest, Ron and I understood that justice for Jordan was not assured, and so we wanted to get our story out there, to shed light on the tricky beast that was Stand Your Ground. In this context, appearing on a national news program like *The Last Word* was an opportunity not to be passed up.

The way we'd come to Lawrence O'Donnell's attention was pure serendipity, which to my mind is another way of saying it was orchestrated by God. In this case, God's emissary was my fellow flight attendant Gary Scales, who had noticed the newsman on his flight. He asked O'Donnell if he happened to have heard about the loud music case, in which his friend's son had been murdered. O'Donnell knew nothing of the story, and as Gary described the events he became very still. When Gary was done, O'Donnell gave my friend his contact information and asked him to let Ron and me know he would be calling us; he wanted us to appear on his show.

I made plans to travel to New York with my girlfriend Lisa White from church. We would overnight in the city and return home following the taping the next morning. After checking into our Midtown hotel, we wandered the streets and avenues. I remember feeling as if I needed space to breathe, as if the throngs of people in the city were pressing in on me. I still hadn't shed the feeling of living in a haze, and that nothing I was experiencing was real. My spirit felt as it was floating in a dimension that was not of this world. It was as if my body was present, walking arm in arm with Lisa up Fifth Avenue, but the essence of who I was, the upbeat, optimistic woman I had once been, was adrift in some other place. I felt disconnected from myself, which I'm sure was my mind's way of protecting me from the full onslaught of losing Jordan.

Lisa and I ended up on the steps of St. Patrick's Cathedral at Fiftieth Street. Standing on the sidewalk, looking up at the soaring Gothic Revival spires, I felt a strong urge to push open the massive bronze doors and go inside. We were met with long rows of candles right as we entered the church, hundreds of little lights, flickering. People kept coming in off the street and lighting more candles, then heading to the pews to pray. There were so many people inside the church, tourists with cameras lifted to their faces, tour groups ushered by guides speaking in hushed tones, individuals gazing upward, awestruck by the magnificent architecture of the sanctuary.

In front of us, a long center aisle led to the beautiful nave with its famous rose window at the far end of the cathedral. On either side of us, wooden pews were dwarfed by towering columns, and watched over by statues of saints. Lisa, sensing the emotion welling up inside me, tapped my shoulder sympathetically and went off to explore on her own. I stood rooted in the middle of the center aisle, my eyes fixed on the white stone altar ahead of me. I began to walk toward it, my legs wooden and my mind in a daze. Halfway there, my whole body suddenly felt weak, unable to bear me up, and I fell to my knees in the nearest pew.

Heavy guttural cries broke from me, the sound like something primal, but this was nothing like the grief that had held me in its fist for weeks. Kneeling in that resplendent place, my hands gripping the pew in front of me, I felt as if something bitter and hard inside me was being dissolved, as if I was being cleansed by my tears. And then I thought I heard the whisper of the Holy Spirit, and I struggled to quiet my heaving sobs in order to tune in more closely. The idea that filled me then was that God wanted me to forgive the man who had taken the life of my son.

"Lord," I sobbed, "how can I forgive him? How do you forgive someone for what he did?"

An image rose in my mind of Jesus on the cross, sacrificing himself for our sins. Still, my spirit wrestled with God.

"Lord," I pleaded, "how can I forgive this evil?"

The response came back to me as a distinct thought.

You must forgive.

God was telling me that I could not move forward in his grace unless I was willing to release my son's killer to his judgment. I had to stop feeding the albatross of bitterness and blame. It was not mine to carry. I needed to set myself free.

Lord, I will try.

Almost as soon as I surrendered, the vast sanctuary was flooded with light, as if the sun outside had emerged from behind a cloud and was pouring its radiance through the tall stained-glass windows on either side of me. The light splashed down over my shoulders and clasped hands, jewel colors floating on the beams, chasing the darkness that had stalked me since that terrible night. And for the first time since my beloved child departed this earth, I felt not fragmented and lost, but *found*.

During the taping with Lawrence O'Donnell the next morning, Ron and I talked about Stand Your Ground and the way it hinged on the perception of fear versus credible threat. As we spoke, I began to grasp that God had been holding a great purpose in store for me all these years. I was to help safeguard the lives of his children, and the way I would do that was by sharing what had happened to my son and by fighting to repeal Stand Your Ground. I knew then why God had asked that I forgive my son's killer. My bitterness and anger were a distraction; they weakened me. Jordan's death had marked the end of the life I knew, a complete erasure of the future I had dreamed, but now I saw that a new beginning was still possible for me. Through God's grace, and for his purpose, I could yet be reborn.

———

The very next morning, December 14, 2012, the gun control debate exploded to the forefront of the nation's consciousness. In Newtown, Connecticut, a mentally disturbed twenty-year-old walked into Sandy Hook Elementary School with a Bushmaster semiautomatic rifle and gunned down twenty children and six teachers. I heard the news as I stood in line at the airport in New York, waiting to board my flight back to Atlanta. It was a long, blurry plane ride. In my living room that night, I could barely sit through the howls of anguish from those children's parents, playing on my television screen. I understood their pain so completely I could barely contain my own.

President Obama had traveled to Newtown to address the devastated community. "The majority of those who died today were children—beautiful little kids between the ages of five and ten years old," he said during a prayer vigil for the Sandy Hook parents. His voice wavered, and he wiped tears from his eyes. "They had their entire lives ahead of them—birthdays, graduations, weddings, kids of their own," he continued. "So our hearts are broken today."

At least I had Jordan for seventeen years, I thought. I was suddenly and unexpectedly flushed with gratitude for the time we'd had, rather than intense regret for the years we'd lost. And there was something else, too, an emerging vision of my future that had been growing clearer ever since I had knelt in St. Patrick's Cathedral the afternoon before.

Two days later, when Obama again addressed the nation, I hung on his words: "We can't tolerate this anymore," he said. "These tragedies must end. And to end them, we must change. We will be told that the causes of such violence are complex, and that is true. No single law, no set of laws can eliminate evil from the world or prevent every senseless act of violence in our society.

"But that can't be an excuse for inaction. . . . We can't accept events like this as routine. Are we really prepared to say that we're powerless in the face of such carnage, that the politics are too hard?"[1]

As the president grieved with the families of Newtown, and beseeched the nation to confront our deadly infatuation with guns, my understanding of the true nature of my own struggle finally clicked into place. Watching Newtown's families weeping over their children, I remembered what Trayvon's father had said about the club to which no parent would choose to belong. Our club grew in membership every single day in America. And it was not comprised solely of the families of young black men like Jordan and Trayvon.

In the weeks since my son's death, I had been laser-focused on how laws like Stand Your Ground rendered young black men in particular vulnerable to death by firearm. I still fervently intended to challenge this law as a way to help safeguard communities of color. But now I saw that my lens would have to grow wider; my view would need to encompass a much larger target, because the massacre at Sandy Hook had nothing to do with race. The shooter and most of his victims were white. But what the Newtown shooting had in common with Jordan's was that it, too, was made possible by our nation's perilously lenient gun laws. In Newtown, these laws had allowed an arsenal of deadly weapons to be readily available to a severely mentally unbalanced young man.

The enormity of the struggle to transform not just dangerous laws, but also the attitudes about guns that had made America such a tinderbox of violence, was finally clear to me. *What can I do to change this?* I wondered in the painful aftershock of Newtown. I had no idea. Alone in my living room, I turned it over to God. *Use me, Lord,* I prayed. *I am your vessel. Show me what you would have me do.*

———

After that, everything started moving at warp speed. First, Minette Nelson, a filmmaker from San Francisco, reached out to Ron and me with a proposal to document our fight to get justice for our boy. She explained that her sixteen-year-old son had alerted her to our story, after reading an article about Jordan in *Rolling Stone*. Minette thought the case had much to teach America about the pitfalls of Stand Your Ground. And so Ron and I agreed to work with her and director Marc Silver on the documentary. The working title was *3½ Minutes*, the length of time it had taken for a conflict over loud music to escalate and become deadly.

Having been cruelly educated by the way Trayvon was vilified and demonized, we were motivated in part by the opportunity to exert some control over the public narrative about our son. Perhaps his case would provoke conversations in people's living rooms, in their churches and classrooms, about unconscious bias and overt prejudice and how they magnified the perils of Stand Your Ground for young black men. This film had the potential to bring home to people that what happened to Jordan was not some isolated tragedy that had nothing to do with them. The nation's lenient gun laws put their loved ones in danger, too. If we could get that message across to the film's audience, we just might convince them to help us bring about change.

The change I was most focused on in the weeks and months after burying my son was the dismantling of Stand Your Ground in each of the twenty-four states in which it had been adopted. I knew the most effective approach would be to seek repeal of the law at the federal level. With this in mind, I traveled to Washington, DC, in the spring of 2013 to meet with Senator Richard Durbin, a Democrat from Illinois. Senator Durbin planned to hold congressional hearings on the dangers of Stand Your Ground, and he was hoping I would testify. In our meeting, I agreed to appear before his congressional committee later in the year to share what had happened to Jordan. Had Michael Dunn had a duty to retreat, I would point out, the outcome of the loud music conflict might have been very different. My son might still be alive.

As I was leaving Senator Durbin's office with my lawyer, John Phillips, that day, I encountered a cluster of women standing outside. They were the senator's next appointment. I recognized one of the women at the same moment she recognized me.

"You're Shannon Watts," I greeted her, extending my hand.

"Lucia McBath," she responded. "You're Jordan Davis's mother."

"Thank you for the work you've been doing for all of us," I said, referring to her efforts as the founder of Moms Demand Action for Gun Sense in America.

Although I didn't yet realize it, that afternoon in Washington, DC, would prove to be a turning point in my life as an activist. Not only would I continue to oppose Stand Your Ground, offering my testimony on the congressional stage, but my recent epiphany that my lens would have to be more expansive was about to come into play.

CHAPTER 14

Every Mom

AT A LOCAL FIRING RANGE, the members of Open Carry Texas had set up a female mannequin, naked from the waist up, her hands in the air. For sixty ear-splitting seconds, men with guns pulverized the female figure with continuous blasts. They called it a "mad minute." When the rapid-fire died down, the men whooped and brandished their weapons, posing for photos beside the bullet-pocked mannequin, her arms now blown off and pants down around her ankles. Their intent was clear. The mad-minute video, later posted on YouTube, was meant to intimidate supporters of Moms Demand Action, the gun violence prevention campaign that had spread across the country in the aftermath of Sandy Hook. The men of Open Carry Texas referred to the group as "mad moms." They and fellow gun rights extremists routinely targeted the women, spitting on Moms in airports, publishing their home addresses and phone numbers online, threatening rape, dismemberment, and worse.[1]

The National Rifle Association at first denounced the mad-minute video, but when infuriated Open Carry Texas supporters made a public show of cutting up their NRA membership cards, the leadership quickly backpedaled, issuing an apology. On social media, Moms supporters hammered the NRA for siding with armed men who openly tried to terrorize mothers—not a good look. As one pro-gun strategist put it, "Moms trump guns."[2]

Shannon Watts was used to such tactics. An Indianapolis-based mother of five and former public relations executive, she'd created a Facebook page calling for mothers everywhere to protest the nation's inadequate gun laws. "As a mom, I can no longer sit on the sidelines," she had written in the days after the massacre at Sandy Hook Elementary in Newtown, Connecticut. "I am too sad and too angry. Don't let anyone tell you we can't talk about this tragedy now—they said the same after Virginia Tech, Gabby Giffords, and Aurora. The time is now."[3]

Shannon, then forty-one, understood the giant she was taking on, but believed that her network could be David to the NRA's Goliath, much as Mothers Against Drunk Driving (MADD) had managed to sway public opinion and change the laws related to drunk drivers in the 1980s. "Change will require action by angry Americans outside of Washington, D.C.," Shannon wrote. "Join us—we will need strength in numbers against a resourceful, powerful and intransigent gun lobby."

Just days later, over a Skype call, she and five other women established the first chapter of Moms Demand Action for Gun Sense in America. Their grassroots effort would quickly grow into a national juggernaut with chapters in every state supported by millions of dollars in private funding. Almost at once, the group began lobbying retailers and restaurant chains across the country to adopt a policy of no guns on their premises. Shannon and her cadre of Moms used social media tools strategically, creating alliterative hashtags to drum up widespread support for their initiatives.

When pro-gun activists made a point of open carrying weapons inside Starbucks in the states where it was legal to do so, for example, Moms Demand Action launched a #SkipStarbucks campaign, with former customers posting pictures of themselves drinking their coffee elsewhere. "As mothers, we wonder why the company is willing to put children and families in so much danger," the group wrote. "Nobody needs to be armed to get a cup of coffee." The grassroots campaign drew the support of some 5.5 million vocal social media users, and 40,000 signed a petition boycotting Starbucks. Less than four months later, Starbucks announced that guns would no longer be allowed in any of its stores.

Moms Demand Action specialized in rattling giant corporate entities through campaigns amplified by social media. In addition to Starbucks, it took on Chipotle (#BurritosNotBullets), Chili's (#RibsNotRifles), and Sonic (#ShakesNotShotguns), all of which outlawed guns on their premises within two weeks of Moms taking aim. The group would prove especially effective when it came to rallying public outcry against companies eager to protect their brands. With efforts to reform gun laws stalling in Congress, the drive to sway public opinion was an inspired strategy, a way to shift the national feeling about firearm safety. When Second Amendment activists responded with menacing displays of firepower, bringing semiautomatic rifles into eating establishments where Moms had gathered for planning meetings, the Moms were unfazed: they took pictures of the glowering men strutting with assault weapons in the midst of family diners, and disseminated them widely as further evidence of the need to protect citizens.

Moms Demand Action would turbocharge its national reach when, in December of 2013 the group joined forces with Mayors Against Illegal Guns, an advocacy group founded by corporate billionaire and former New York mayor Michael Bloomberg. The Mayors had deep pockets, political connections, and extensive experience in policy-making, while the Moms had a national network of activists that everyone in America could get behind—mothers. Four months later, the two groups combined their strengths to launch Everytown for Gun Safety, and prepared to meet the NRA on the legislative playing field it had dominated for going on three decades.

Under the umbrella of Everytown, the Mayors worked mostly inside the political arena while the Moms continued their public advocacy, for example, forcing Facebook to more closely monitor private gun sales on its platform, which allowed buyers to circumvent background checks. Next, the mothers protested Target's open-carry policy in stores, where men in camouflage with loaded assault rifles browsed alongside family shoppers. As part of Everytown, the moms were now backed by some fifty million dollars in annual funding, and their mailing list had expanded to a million and a half names. Utilizing these new resources, they inundated Target headquarters with tens of thousands of phone calls, collected hundreds of thousands of signers on petitions, and staged "stroller jams" in shopping aisles. Target soon announced that guns would no longer be allowed in its 1,834 stores nationwide.

These significant early victories went a long way toward transforming public opinion about America's gun culture. "Changes to the culture are more important in some ways than legal changes," noted Mark Glaze, former executive director of Everytown. "This sends a message that having guns everywhere makes people uncomfortable, which goes directly against the gun lobby's agenda—to normalize having them everywhere."[4]

While Shannon Watts and the other Moms took pains to point out they were not anti-gun, just anti–gun violence, many received phone calls threatening rape and murder. Despite the intimidation tactics from pro-gun factions, the Moms refused to back down. Instead they ramped up their campaign by taking on the avoidable tragedy of unintentional gun deaths, especially in cases where children were harmed by the careless storage of firearms. In 2013 alone, 100 children were killed in unintentional shootings after gaining access to loaded guns.[5] Shannon Watts argued the gun owners in such cases should be prosecuted. "This idea of 'accidental' gun deaths, when something is truly negligence, has to be remedied," she said.[6]

Moms and Everytown also fought to keep guns out of schools, bars, and entertainment venues by agitating for "social responsibility" laws. In addition, Everytown mobilized to close background check loopholes that allow guns to be acquired by domestic abusers. Research has shown that when a gun is easily accessible in any kind of household conflict, women are five times more likely to end up dead.[7] Further, a common characteristic of the majority of mass shooters is a history of domestic violence, with 54 percent of mass shooting events targeting a spouse, ex-spouse, or relative.[8]

Everytown's overarching goal now is to support individuals for political office who will commit to agitating for commonsense gun laws. And this is not a partisan effort: both Republicans and Democrats stand to benefit from the organization's hefty donations to the campaigns of those who advocate for gun safety—and both will be held to account. By wielding the immense power of the purse, Moms and Everytown have swarmed onto the battlefield of electoral politics to beat the NRA at their own game.

―――

My own meeting with Shannon Watts and the other Moms in Washington, DC, was fortuitous. Within the week, I joined the group as a spokesperson for gun-violence prevention. In that capacity, I began to tell Jordan's story at rallies, to meet with legislators in state houses, and to help raise awareness about gun safety issues and the dangerous political agenda of the gun lobby. Requests for me to speak poured in, with practically no effort on my part. I had no doubt God was the architect. One morning, while I was on my knees in prayer, the Lord came through to me with clarity: *Through you, my people must see my face.* In the weeks and months that followed, I tried to live in the consciousness of God's will. On every stage, before I spoke, I bowed my head, clasped my hands, and whispered, "Lord, keep my heart pure and guide my words, and shower everyone here present with your grace."

I knew that sharing my personal testimony as a mother would allow people to grasp the tragedy of gun violence in a more intimate way. As Chuck Hurley, a former CEO of MADD had observed, "There's no way people can understand 30,000 firearm deaths. The bigger the number, the less real it is."[9] But a mother losing her only son in such a senseless and easily preventable manner—people could imagine what it might feel like to walk in those shoes. They could begin to fathom the depth of heartbreak.

When Curtis begged me to slow down—I was still working for Delta while doing speaking engagements in far-flung cities on my days off—I assured him that my schedule, rather than draining me, had filled me with renewed purpose. That alone was proof of God's design, I told him. That night, I took my dear husband's hands in mine and asked him to walk with me for Jordan's sake, and to trust that our Heavenly Father would bring us through.

PART THREE

AWAKENING

CHAPTER 15

A Long-Held Secret

AS I TRAVELED ALL OVER the country to speak about firearm safety, my public face was now that of a mother who has lost her only child to gun violence. This was the woman the world saw when I stepped on stage or spoke from their television screens. My audiences had no clue of a more private pain about which I had seldom spoken. They could not know that Jordan was not the first child I had lost, or that his death now had made that decades-old secret harder than ever to bear.

At fifteen, I had become pregnant by a boy who lived in my neighborhood. He was a couple of years older than me, and it happened the very first time I ever had sex. I couldn't figure out at first why my cheerleading uniform was getting so snug across the belly, or why my shirt buttons had started to strain across my chest. It couldn't be that I was getting fat because I was hardly eating anything; I was nauseous all the time. Confused, I started wearing my mother's shirts, leaving them untucked to cover where I had left the very top of my skirt zipper open. I didn't have a clue what was going on until the night I threw up at the dinner table.

The meal that evening was hot dogs and French fries. As my mother, Lori, and I ate together in our small kitchen, the smell of the food began to overwhelm me. Suddenly I was retching all over myself. Mom jumped up, alarmed, and guided me to the bathroom. She pressed one hand against my perspiring brow as I puked up everything I had eaten, and when I was done, she smoothed my hair back from my face as I brushed my teeth and rinsed my mouth. In the mirror above the sink, our eyes met, and in that moment, I saw what my mother knew. Strange as it seems, it was only then, seeing the truth in her indescribably sad eyes that I understood I was with child.

The next thing I remember is the two of us sitting on the couch in our living room. My mother had pulled me onto her lap, and she held me against her shoulder, both of us crying softly. Next to us, my twelve-year-old sister was bawling her eyes out, making more noise than Mom and me, even though she had no idea what was happening.

"When?" my mother asked me.

I could only shrug listlessly inside the circle of her arms.

"Who was it?" she wanted to know.

I told her the name of the boy.

My mother closed her eyes as if praying for strength, while rocking me back and forth on her lap like a little girl.

"I'm sorry I didn't do a better job as your mother," she said at last.

"Mom, you did fine," I mumbled, my face pressed against her shoulder. I felt her deep sigh, and wanted so much to comfort her, but the truth was I had no idea how to soften the blow I had dealt. My mother seemed so defeated.

After a long while, she stood me up from her lap and the competent mother I had always known returned. "Okay," she said, "we'll have to get you to the doctor, figure out how far along you are, and

find out what we need to do to make sure you have a healthy baby."
She sounded almost matter-of-fact now. A panic rose in me. In the
wake of my father's abandonment of the family, I knew how hard
Mom was working for the three of us, picking up extra shifts at the
hospital to make ends meet while she studied for her master's degree
in nursing administration. It was why she was blaming herself. She
believed that if she had been home with us more, providing supervi-
sion and oversight, this would not have happened.

My shame was immeasurable. I was America's stereotype of the
unwed pregnant black teen being raised by a single mother and bent
on repeating the cycle. My mom was convinced she had failed me,
which to me was evidence that I had failed her.

"Mom," I whispered, "we have to make sure the baby has a good
home." I knew I was ill equipped to give the little one what he or she
would need to thrive. I was a child myself, not even mature enough to
recognize my own pregnancy. And yet I didn't want to have an abortion. I was so afraid of what came next. What was I going to do?

"Shhhh," Mom said, placing her finger over my lips. "Right now
we just have to make sure you and the baby are fine, and then we'll
get you some counseling, and from there we'll figure out the rest."

——————

Without ever discussing it, Mom, Lori, and I decided not to tell
Daddy. My father went to his grave not knowing what transpired
for me that year. I was approaching the end of tenth grade, and
the gynecologist my mother took me to had assessed me to be four
months along. I carefully disguised my expanding belly until school
let out in June. The next day, Mom packed Lori and me into her car
and drove us to a neighboring state where I was to live in a Catholic

home for pregnant teens until I delivered my baby. We were assured the child would be placed with a loving family in a private Christian adoption.

The home for pregnant girls looked completely nondescript from the outside, a boxy, concrete building painted an indeterminate shade of beige. There were no trees or sprawling grounds like you see in the movies, just a sidewalk and a frosted-glass door leading to the reception area. From there, a long hallway ran past offices, counseling rooms, and medical exam rooms, opening onto a large communal area where teenage girls, some black, some white, most of them visibly pregnant, lounged on the couches, reading magazines or watching television with blank faces. They looked up at me as I entered, then looked away. I understood they were as scared and lost as I was. Off to the left was a large cafeteria with white tile walls to the ceiling, white Formica tables, and white plastic molded chairs. Beyond that, lined up along a corridor, were dormitory-type rooms with two beds each. For the next four to five months, this was to be my home.

I would soon discover that, despite the severe institutional appearance of the surroundings, the nuns who ran the residence were warm and nurturing. They counseled the girls kindly, and scheduled academic classes on weekday mornings so that we wouldn't fall behind in school. And of course, we had regular medical check-ups to make sure our babies were progressing well. On Sundays, we all knelt together in the chapel and prayed that our babies would have a good life.

There were about twenty of us in residence at a time, and while we knew what was planned for our newborns, we had no idea what lay ahead for ourselves. A shell-shocked air of despondency permeated that place; it felt like shame threaded through with loneliness and fear. My own apprehensions were amplified by the awareness that my pregnancy had just about broken my mother. "I tried so hard to protect you," she had told me. "I tried to make sure you were safe and had all the same privileges your father would have given you if he'd been there."

My sense of having disgraced the family had only deepened when we sat down with the boy and his parents a few days after my first gynecologist appointment back in Joliet. Their only contribution had been to suggest that I terminate the pregnancy. "I see," my mother said with pursed lips and narrowed eyes. We left soon after, and never spoke to any of them again.

In counseling sessions at the residence, the nuns tried to get me to talk about my feelings toward the boy who had got me pregnant and walked away. I was angry for sure. It felt so unfair, but I tucked those feelings deep inside and refused to explore them with anyone. I didn't see what good could come of dwelling on a boy I intended to have nothing to do with in the future. Instead, I tried to figure out how I might console my mother. More than anything else, it was her regret and sorrow I felt driven to repair.

As I came to term that fall, the doctors at the residence scheduled a date on which to induce labor. My mother and sister drove from Joliet to be with me for the birth. The doctors and nurses put me to sleep and delivered my child using forceps. They woke me up immediately after.

"You have a beautiful baby girl," a nurse told me as she placed on my chest a squirming bundle tightly swaddled in a soft white blanket with pink and green stripes. I moved my daughter to the crook of my arm and gazed down at her perfect, button face framed by a mass of curly black hair. Her nose was her father's, and her skin was the same honey-brown color as my own. My heart swelled with love and pain. I could hardly take in the miracle my body had nurtured to life; I was confused; I was desolate; I was ashamed. How would I give her up? Was there really no other way? Tears squeezed from the corners of my eyes because I wanted so powerfully to keep her, to let her know how much I already loved her. And yet I knew I couldn't. My mother was raising Lori and me alone. There was no way we would be able to give this baby all she would need. *I* couldn't give this child all she would need.

My thoughts swirled darkly as the nurse took my little girl from my arms a few moments later, and an orderly wheeled me out of the delivery room and into recovery. And that was it. Because the adoption was closed, I never knew anything about the family with whom my baby had been placed. I didn't even know until years later that my mother and sister had held my daughter in the next room before the Christian social workers took her away.

The three of us drove home to Joliet in a car heavy with silence, and the following Monday I returned to school. I was in eleventh grade now, and although rumors drifted around me from time to time, I never talked about the baby daughter I'd delivered in a state that was not my own. I had left a piece of my heart there, but apart from my mother and sister, and much later my husbands, no one would ever know.

My mother would say, "Are you okay, Lou? Do you need to talk about anything?"

I'd just shake my head, traumatized by the loss I was feeling but not knowing any other way to cope but in silence. Decades later, when Jordan was taken from me, that first loss only intensified the second.

I remembered how, when I was trying to conceive Jordan and was having so much trouble carrying to term, I'd wondered if God was punishing me. I thought that perhaps I didn't deserve to be a mother. I prayed: *God, if this is your will, I accept it*. And then Jordan was born, and I had felt as if God was giving me another chance. It's part of the reason I channeled so much into him from the start. I wanted to do right by him. And I wanted to praise and thank my Heavenly Father for my son's presence by raising him to love God above all else.

When Jordan and I found Trinity Chapel, we grew even deeper in faith. And after Jordan died, this community saved me. As angry as I was at God for taking Jordan from me, I didn't for a moment think he was punishing me. I knew by then that God didn't work that way. More likely, Jordan had been given his earthly assignment before he was ever born. I understand now that Jordan was never truly mine; he was a gift from God, entrusted to me only for a time. It comforts me sometimes to think that in much the same way, God had chosen me to deliver to another family a beautiful and perfect baby girl. But that doesn't mean I did not ache at losing her.

Now, with Jordan so violently torn from me, that first loss assailed me like a fresh wound, all the more raw because I could not publicly acknowledge its existence. All I could do was pray for the baby I had delivered into someone else's care; indeed, I had prayed for her every single day of our lives since giving birth to her on a blustery autumn afternoon. And now, everywhere I went, even as I stood before the world as a mother grieving the loss of her only child, I peered into the faces of young women of a certain age, and I wondered: *Are you my little girl? Are you safe and happy? Have you had a good life?*

CHAPTER 16

The Color of Justice

THE FIRST TIME I SAW Sybrina Fulton, she was standing in the green room backstage at the Black Male Re-Imagined II conference in New York City. It was one week to the day after the first anniversary of the death of her son, Trayvon, and one month after what would have been his eighteenth birthday. Star Jones, the lawyer and television commentator, was scheduled to interview Sybrina on stage about how public perception had shaped the way her son's case had unfolded. I was not scheduled to speak at the conference, but, along with my attorney, John Phillips, I had been invited to attend.

Someone, I don't recall whom, took my arm and guided me across the room to be introduced to Sybrina. She was tall and graceful, and supremely composed, but I knew that just like me, inside she was a pool of tears. Indeed, the moment our eyes met, our carefully marshaled defenses crumbled. "You are the only person in this room who knows what I feel," I whispered as Sybrina hugged me. When she pulled back, I saw that her eyes were brimming. She smiled sadly.

"We know," she agreed. "Oh, we know."

Sybrina and I didn't see each other again for several months, but we traveled similar paths during that time. We were both constantly on the road, crisscrossing the nation to testify about the violence that had stolen our children. Trayvon's parents were also at the center of the burgeoning Black Lives Matter movement. Their son's name had become a rallying cry for racial justice, his young face staring out from the iconic hoodie now embedded in the nation's consciousness.

Four months later on July 13, 2013, the news broke that Trayvon's killer had been acquitted of all charges. The verdict felt like a knife being twisted in my heart. I could not begin to grasp how Sybrina and Tracy survived it. Immediately after the acquittal, news commentator Melissa Harris-Perry asserted that the case had been entirely about race. As proof, she cited the fear and sadness black families were feeling that day, and the fact that Trayvon Martin, a black teen with no criminal record, had been effectively tried and convicted for his own murder. Even worse was the dehumanizing stereotype of Trayvon that the defense had put forward. They had transformed an innocent child walking home from the store into the scary black bogeyman of white America's nightmares.

But perhaps the most distressing aspect of the trial was that the verdict had been almost expected. As journalist and author Jelani Cobb wrote in the *New Yorker*: "The familiarity dulled the sharp edges of the tragedy. The decision the six jurors reached on Saturday evening will inspire anger, frustration, and despair, but little surprise, and this is the most deeply saddening aspect of the entire affair. From the outset—throughout the forty-four days it took for there to be an arrest, and then in the sixteen months it took for the case to come to trial—there was a nagging suspicion that it would culminate in disappointment. Call this historical profiling."[1]

Obviously, I won't attempt to relitigate the case here, but I will say its outcome made me despair of ever getting justice for Jordan. Our attorney, in an effort to bolster our spirits, reminded us that only two people really knew what had happened the night Trayvon was killed, and one of them was dead. In contrast, dozens of witnesses saw Michael Dunn shooting at my son and his friends. John Phillips had already won civil settlements in wrongful death and defamation proceedings against Dunn, and he was confident that we stood a good chance of conviction in a criminal trial. Still, I worried. Our case, like Trayvon's, rested on the jury's assessment of the validity of the killer's self-defense claim. The racial subtext was inescapable.

When Duval County state attorney Angela Corey told the press that her office was preparing to try Michael Dunn for first-degree murder in the shooting death of Jordan Davis, many suspected the timing of her announcement was intended to distract from the firestorm of criticism she was receiving over the acquittal of Trayvon's killer. She had been appointed special prosecutor in that case. I chose not to look too deeply into her motivations as I welcomed the news that Jordan would have his day in court. Ron and I hoped to find some measure of closure not just for our family but also for Sybrina Fulton and Tracy Martin. A conviction for the murder of our son would mean a rejection of his killer's self-defense claim. It would also offer stark testimony on how brutally misguided the application of the Stand Your Ground doctrine had been. Even more, for all those African American families who had seen their loved ones' killers walk free, a conviction in the murder of Jordan Davis would affirm that in the United States, a black child's life had value.

––––––

Michael Dunn was worried about the jury. "My fear is that [if] I get one black on my jury it will be a mistrial as I am convinced they are racially biased against me," he wrote to a family member from jail. He seemed convinced that a black juror would be incapable of objectively assessing the evidence. On the other hand, he appeared to believe that an all-white jury would side with him and send him home. "White folks who live here are pretty much anti-black," he told his fiancée, Rhonda Rouer, in a June 14, 2013, letter.[2] Dunn and our lawyers agreed on one thing: the composition of the jury would be crucial to the outcome of the case.

Curtis and I flew from Atlanta to Jacksonville on Monday, February 3, 2014, for the criminal trial. Dunn had been charged with one count of first-degree murder, three counts of attempted first-degree murder, and one count of shooting into "an occupied dwelling," Tommie Stornes's car.

By Thursday afternoon, the jury had been impaneled. Sitting next to Curtis, Ron, and Carolina in the courtroom, I peered into the faces of the four white women, four white men, two black women, one Asian woman, and one Hispanic man who would be our jurors. I tried to imagine who they might be in their lives away from the jury box. How many of them were parents? Now the presiding judge, Russell L. Healey, was talking to them about how the trial would be conducted and how they should assess the evidence. My breaths were shallow with anxiety and anticipation as the judge wrapped up his instructions and Assistant State Attorney John Guy rose from the prosecution table to deliver his opening statement.

He began by setting the scene outside the convenience store, recounting the argument over loud music, and relating how Dunn, incensed at Jordan's insubordination, had pulled out his legally owned Taurus 9-millimeter pistol and pumped ten bullets into a car full of teenagers, not a single one of them armed. When the shooting stopped, he said, Jordan was gasping for air, his head in Leland Brunson's lap. One bullet had penetrated his right leg; another lodged in his left leg. But it was the third bullet that did the most damage. The prosecutor described how it had pierced Jordan's right side, tore through his liver, passed through both of his lungs, and shredded his aorta.

"And then the blood that for seventeen years had run so naturally through Jordan Davis's veins and arteries, was pouring out of him," Guy said, pausing to allow the jury to absorb his words. "Michael David Dunn pointed a semiautomatic pistol at four unarmed kids from a distance much closer than you and I," he continued. "And then drove off. He didn't call the police. He went to his hotel with his girlfriend and he called a pizza-delivery man, and ordered pizza. He took his little dog for a walk outside the hotel, turned on a movie, and made himself a big, tall drink, rum and Coke. And not long after an emergency doctor at Shands Hospital pronounced Jordan Davis dead, that defendant put his head on his hotel pillow and went to sleep."

I had heard these details a thousand times, but now I tried to process them as the jury might. Certainly, Dunn's actions after the shooting appeared callous. If he had felt that his life was in danger, and that shooting into Tommie's car was necessary to defend himself, why hadn't he immediately called the police?

Prosecutor John Guy went on to preemptively refute several points that he knew the defense would try to make stick. For starters, Dunn had claimed that Jordan was getting out of the car and coming toward him in a menacing way, forcing him to reach for his gun. Guy assured the jurors that the trajectory of the bullets as they drilled through the door of the Durango and entered Jordan's body would prove beyond any shadow of a doubt that when Dunn opened fire, Jordan was seated in the back seat of the SUV with the door closed, and nothing in his hands. In fact, the physical evidence showed that Jordan had been leaning *away* from the defendant, toward Leland, possibly trying to move out of harm's way.

Dunn's criminal defense lawyer, Cory Strolla, addressed the jury next. It was immediately clear that he intended to rely on two tactics for creating reasonable doubt—turn the victim into the antagonist and accuse the police of an inept and bungled investigation. Strolla insisted that Jordan had pointed a gun at Dunn, and that the boys had ditched it when Tommie brought the car to a stop in the adjacent parking lot. He argued that no weapon was ever found because police neglected to search the area until four days later. Apart from the fact that Ron and I knew with certainty that there had been no guns in the car, the idea that the boys were armed never made sense to us. If they had been, wouldn't they have tried to defend themselves when Dunn opened fire? And yet not a single answering shot came from Tommie's car. So why did Dunn keep shooting as the terrified boys backed away, when dozens of witnesses could see he was clearly not in any danger?

And another thing: Cory Strolla made much of the notion that the music in Tommie's car was so loud that the boys couldn't hear what Jordan said to Michael Dunn. This was to counter the boys' testimony that Jordan had never issued any threats. And yet Strolla argued that Michael Dunn, sitting in another car, had heard Jordan say, "You're dead bitch! This shit's going down now, bitch!" as he pointed a gun out the back window of the Durango. You can't have it both ways: you can't assert the other three boys didn't hear Jordan intimidate Dunn because of the volume of the music, yet Dunn—who we would learn was deaf in one ear—heard him clearly over the thumping baseline.

The defense, it appeared, was just throwing everything at the wall, hoping they could cause enough confusion to foster reasonable doubt. Though Strolla strained to portray Jordan and his friends as America's nightmare of black criminality, I was encouraged by how calm and credible Leland, Tommie, and Tevin were on the witness stand, even as Strolla aggressively peppered them with questions, trying to undermine their composure, trying to get them to admit to things that hadn't happened, like getting rid of a gun. Their courteous presence and steady testimony gave the lie to the defense's attempt to characterize them as hardened thugs. But Jordan was not there to account for himself.

I worried that he might exist for the jury only in the competing portraits presented by the prosecution and the defense. Which sense of Jordan would lodge more deeply in the jurors' minds? How hard would they work to see the truth of who my son had been through their own rooted biases about young black men? How I wished the men and women in the jury box could have known Jordan, his compassion, humor, and light. Throughout the painful back and forth, I sat in the courtroom hugging myself, literally holding myself together. Who would the jurors believe?

I dreaded the moment when the state would bring out images of Jordan, slumped and bleeding at the scene. When it came, I got up and left the courtroom, retiring to the family room that had been provided for us. Sitting alone in that chamber, I studied my hands resting in my lap and concentrated on the memory of my son's smile, the easy confidence of his walk, the slope of his shoulders, the bend of his elbows, the map of veins along his forearms. I tried to call back every detail of Jordan in life, blocking out the horrific images of his bullet-ridden body being paraded before the jury.

Reporters from news outlets across the country had crowded into the courtroom, their cameras trained on Dunn, on Ron and me, and on the witnesses. I hoped that the scrutiny of the press would help us secure justice. Outside the courtroom, hundreds of picketers milled around the news network vans, holding handmade signs with slogans like "The only one with a gun was Dunn" and "Will this be another Trayvon?" They'd seen the same news reports as we had, so they knew there was a good chance that Dunn, like Zimmerman, might escape conviction, especially if his fiancée supported his story that the boys had pointed a weapon.

A lot was riding on Rhonda Rouer's testimony. But Shawn Atkins, the young homeless man who had jotted down the Jetta's license plate number, gave me reason to hope. He had been parked three spots over from the boys' SUV, and the sound of gunshots had drawn his attention. On the witness stand, the prosecutor asked Atkins if he'd heard Rouer say anything to Dunn when she got back to the car.

"I didn't hear her say anything but the look on her face said enough," he responded.

"What did the look on her face say to you?" the prosecutor pressed. "Describe it."

"Horror," Atkins said. "Horror."

Two days later, when Rouer introduced herself from the witness stand, her voice quavered. Throughout her testimony, she was never far from tears, and often they overflowed.

"Ms. Rouer, as you got back in the passenger side of the car, did you see a firearm at that time?" the prosecutor asked at one point.

"Yes, Michael was putting it into the glove box."

And later: "While driving back to the hotel, Ms. Rouer, did you ever suggest that the defendant call 911?"

"No," Dunn's fiancée said.

According to Rouer, after she and Dunn returned to their hotel, Dunn went to walk their dog, Charlie, while she changed her clothes. Then she went to sit in the lounge area by the elevators.

"Why did you go out to that sitting area?" the prosecution asked her.

"Because I figured that the police would be there soon."

When law enforcement didn't arrive, Rouer returned to the room where she and Dunn ordered pizza, made two stiff rum and Cokes, and eventually slept. The next morning, they saw on the news that a teenager had been killed in the altercation at the gas station the night before. At that point, Rouer begged Dunn to drive them home to Satellite Beach two and a half hours away. On the witness stand, through sobs, she explained, "I thought I was going to be arrested, too, and I wanted to get Charlie taken care of before that happened."

That she had been waiting for the police to come and take them into custody told me she did not truly believe the shooting had been justified. Unlike the defendant, Rouer appeared to be in anguish. And when the prosecution played a video of her inside the convenience store as the first shots were fired, she broke down completely, forcing the court to pause proceedings until she could regain herself.

On the eighth day, Michael Dunn took the stand. His lawyer asked him if his dog, Charlie, was like his child. Dunn made a show of choking up, blowing his nose, wiping his eyes. I kept my face as neutral as I could but inside I was screaming: *What about my child? Jordan was MY child and you murdered him!* The blood was such a roar inside my head I barely heard when Dunn insisted, as he had all along, that my son had pointed a gun or weapon of some sort and threatened to kill him. He claimed that he had shared this with his fiancée to explain why he'd shot into the boys' vehicle.

On this point, during the trial's rebuttal phase, the prosecution recalled Rhonda Rouer to the stand. I held my breath as the assistant state attorney launched into what was perhaps the trial's most critical line of questioning.

"When you came out of the Gate Gas Station and you got into the defendant's car . . . did the defendant ever tell you he saw a gun in that SUV?" prosecutor Erin Wolfson asked Rouer.

"No," she said.

"Did the defendant ever tell you that he saw a weapon of any kind in that SUV?"

"No."

"There was no mention of a stick?"

"No."

"There was no mention of a shotgun?"

"No."

"There was no mention of a barrel?"

"No."

"There was no mention of a lead pipe?"

"No."

"Back in the hotel room, Ms. Rouer, that same night, did the defendant ever tell you that he saw the boys with a firearm?"

"No."

"Did he ever tell you he saw the boys with a weapon?"

"No."

"On the two hour drive the following morning, did the defendant ever tell you he saw a gun in the SUV?"

"No."

"And on that two hour drive did he ever tell you he saw a weapon of any kind in the SUV?"

"No."

As Rouer stepped down from the witness stand and made her way out of the courtroom, I released a long breath. Whether it was because she was a mother herself, or because she knew deep down that our boys hadn't meant any harm, she didn't lie to protect her fiancé. We still weren't assured of getting the verdict we hoped for but the prosecution had done its part. Now it was up to the jury.

————

Saturday, February 15, 2014, was the day before Jordan would have turned nineteen. That night, the jury told the judge that they had reached a verdict of guilty on four of the five charges, but were hopelessly deadlocked on the first-degree murder charge. Ron and I were dumbfounded: How could Michael Dunn be found guilty of attempting to murder Tommie, Tevin, and Leland, yet not be guilty of actually murdering Jordan in the same incident? It just didn't make sense. I could not help but wonder if my earlier fears had been justified: Perhaps the three boys who had testified in court had become real to the jurors, while Jordan, in his absence, remained just another young black man, an American stereotype of imminent danger, the truth of him elusive to the men and women in the jury box.

"I wish I had something more to say about the fact that Michael Dunn was not convicted for killing a black boy," author Ta-Nehisi Coates wrote in *The Atlantic* after the verdicts were read. "Except I said it after George Zimmerman was not convicted of killing a black boy." His weary tone captured the pervasive mood of African Americans at the trial's outcome—we were angry, saddened, disheartened, and yet we were unsurprised that the criminal justice system had once again sent the message that black lives simply did not matter. Ron and I consoled ourselves that at least Jordan's killer would not walk free. He was facing a minimum of sixty years for the four charges on which the state had won convictions. On the most major charge, the first-degree murder of our son, the judge declared a mistrial.

As we left the courthouse that evening, the crowd of picketers parted quietly to allow us through. "Thank you, thank you," I said, grasping one hand and then another and another. Some people laid hands on us and whispered, "God bless you," as we walked through the demonstrators to our car. The crowd sewed itself back together behind us, and new cries of "Justice for Jordan!" reverberated in the air. I was profoundly grateful for every voice raised in support of my son, and for the way the people of Jacksonville had kept vigil with us throughout the trial. Even though my heart was cracking open inside my chest, I held on to the belief that all was not lost. Jordan's case would be retried, and we would continue to fight for him. We would continue to insist to the world that his life had had meaning. This was how we would love him now.

CHAPTER 17

A Jury of His Peers

THE SECOND TIME AROUND, I didn't miss a single moment of jury selection. I wanted to look into every face and learn all I could about the individuals who might decide our case. I sat in the courtroom, making notes in my journal and praying continuously that God would help us seat a jury able to see past the fears and prejudices that were still waging a centuries-old battle for America's soul.

When, on September 24, 2014, the jury was finally sworn in and sequestered, I was not at all sure that my prayers had been answered. In my journal, I wrote: "I don't believe we will get a conviction. The lawyers have chosen seven white males, three white females, one black female, and one black male. This is our twelve. In this country, with this jury, the odds are against us. Only you, Lord, can move on their hearts."

I was more intensely aware than I had ever been that the outcome of criminal cases rested almost entirely with the makeup of the jury. Lawyers would plead their cases, witnesses would have their say, judges would instruct and guide, but in the end, it was those twelve men and women debating the case around a conference table that would carry the day. For good or ill, each juror brought a kaleidoscope of experiences, beliefs, and attitudes with them, yet the final decision had to be unanimous.

By this time, we had learned that at Michael Dunn's first trial back in February, ten of the twelve jurors had already judged Michael Dunn guilty of all charges when they took the first poll in the jury room. According to Juror No. 4, a white woman named Valerie, only two jurors had thought that the defendant acted in self-defense. During thirty hours of deliberation, heated arguments had ensued, with the two jurors not budging on their position that Dunn had been justified in killing our son. The two jurors eventually convinced a third to join their side, and no amount of further evidence review could change their minds. They did manage to come to agreement on the three attempted murder charges. Valerie explained the verdict on those charges was influenced by the fact that Dunn had exited his car and continued shooting even after the boys had retreated.

"We had a lot of discussion on him getting out of the car," Juror No. 4 told ABC News. "The threat is now gone. And your intent is yet to still go ahead and pursue this vehicle."[1]

On the first and most serious charge of killing Jordan, Valerie felt that the defendant "got away with murder." Of the nine jurors who thought Dunn was guilty, she said, "We all believed there was another way out, another option." The ABC News reporter asked her to name some of the options. Valerie sighed. "Roll your window up," she said. "Ignore the taunting. Put your car in reverse. Back up to the front of the store. Move a parking spot over."[2] I prayed that this time around, everyone on our jury panel would be like Valerie.

Meanwhile, Dunn was continuing to spew bigotry and hate. He had claimed during his testimony at the first trial that he never used the word "thug," yet his letters from jail were peppered with it. "The black community here in Jacksonville is in an uproar against me," he wrote to his grandmother. "The three other thugs that were in the car are telling stories to cover up their true colors."[3] Later, writing to his fiancée, he called black people the "scourge of the country," and said, "The more time I am exposed to these people the more prejudiced against them I become."[4]

In other letters, amid rants about State Attorney Angela Corey and threats to sue Duval County for violating his civil rights, he continued venting his views on African Americans: "If more people would arm themselves and kill these fucking idiots when they're threatening you, eventually they may take the hint and change their behavior," he wrote to his daughter, adding that "eventually, we as a society will wake up and realize that we need to arm ourselves, as the government welfare programs have produced a culture of entitlement for a certain segment of our society."[5]

Interestingly, in the same letter, he complained that a former neighbor had told authorities that his ex-wife had accused Dunn of choking her during their marriage. I watched that interview with the neighbor, Charles Hendrix. It took place on his screened porch and was more than an hour long. Hendrix called Dunn "arrogant and egotistical" with a superior attitude. He also described how not one, but two of Dunn's ex-wives had come over to his house and told him that Dunn had put a gun to their heads and threatened to blow their brains out. Hendrix had persuaded one of the ex-wives to bring the gun to him. He offered to keep it for a while to remove the danger. His neighbor agreed to the plan, but a little while later she asked him to return the gun to her so she could replace it in the home. Hendrix claimed she was terrified that if Dunn found the gun missing, there would be hell to pay.[6]

None of this was admissible in the court trial; I believe it fell into the category of hearsay. But Dunn's propensity for violence was widely reported online, in print journals, and on broadcast news. Would the next jury glimpse this aspect of Michael Dunn during the trial? Would they be able to see past the nation's pervasive stereotype of young black men as thugs, to really assess what had transpired on the evening when I lost my son? Or would they see the defendant as the victim, as Dunn himself insisted he was. "I just can't shake the notion that I'm the rape girl that they're blaming because I was wearing skimpy clothes," he told Rouer in a phone call from jail. "I'm the victim that's being blamed. I refused to be the victim and now I'm being punished for it. I'm not optimistic that those boys will tell the truth."[7]

With Judge Russell L. Healey once again presiding, opening statements were given on Thursday, September 25, 2014. As I shifted closer to Curtis on the hard bench of the courtroom, I reflected that it had been almost two years since Jordan took his final breath. First, Assistant State Attorney John Guy addressed the jury, after which Dunn's new criminal defense attorney, Waffa Hanania, gave her statement. In the days following, the parade of witnesses once again described the night of Black Friday 2012 in excruciating, minute-by-minute detail.

Leland, Tevin, and Tommie were as steady in their testimony as before. I noted their appearances in my journal:

> Sweet Tevin is now taking the stand. I love his tender, smiling spirit. Leland held his own under the cross-examination.
> I am glad to see him doing better. I am so happy Jordan was with his best friend when he died. Tommie is now on the stand. He is emerging to be a fine young man, studying business in college. I am proud of him too. Lord, bless each

of these young men. They are such good kids. I pray they
continue to grow into successful men of society.

During breaks in the proceedings, Curtis and I retreated to the
conference room that had been reserved for family members. So many
people rallied around us, offering love and support. Among them
were Erica Gordon Taylor, a cousin of Emmett Till who had flown
in from Chicago, and Sybrina Fulton, mother of Trayvon, who had
driven down from Sanford. "This isn't just about justice for Jordan,"
Sybrina reminded me. "This is about justice for Trayvon, too."

On the sixth day, the jury retired to deliberate. Pacing restlessly in
the family room, I knew that we might have to wait days for a decision. Yet, after only five-and-a-half hours, the jury sent word to Judge
Healey that they had reached consensus. My heart was galloping as
we filed back into the courtroom to await the reading of the verdict.
To calm myself, I mentally reviewed how the trial had gone, trying to
gauge how each witness's testimony had landed with the jurors. This
time, our attorneys had put more emphasis on Dunn fleeing the scene,
neglecting to call the police, and never mentioning seeing a gun to his
fiancée. All these actions revealed the defendant's consciousness of
guilt, the state argued. On the other hand, the boys' decision to return
to the Gate Gas Station to get help immediately after the shooting, and
the fact that they called and then waited for police, pointed to their
consciousness of innocence.

Prosecutor John Guy had used a phrase in both opening and clos-
ing arguments that stayed with me. Michael Dunn, he said, had killed
my son "with malice in his heart and intent in his aim." Guy then
itemized the series of deliberate actions that Dunn had to take on the
way to fatally shooting Jordan: he had to reach over, open the glove
compartment, un-holster his weapon, take it out of the glove box,

cock it, aim it, and pull the trigger. All of this added up to premeditation, our lawyers argued, which defined first-degree murder.

Now, as we waited for the verdict, I believed the state had presented its strongest case. Yet when the jury forewoman announced a verdict of guilty, I was stunned. Beside me, Ron gasped, and then we both hung our heads and cried. So many emotions were rushing through me I couldn't identify them all. But the feelings that were strongest of all were relief and gratitude. And even though my child was dead, even though the sorrow of that would never leave me, there was also jubilation. "Jordan, we did it," I whispered, lifting my eyes and my palms heavenward. "We got you justice after all."

———

People often ask: Why do you think Jordan's killer was convicted when so many white men who murder black boys walk free? Even more remarkable, how did the state manage to convince a jury of mostly white men to convict another white man for fatally shooting a young black man? That is a rare thing in America, but in Jacksonville, Florida, on October 1, 2014, we defied the odds.

The factors underlying our victory were both situational and strategic. Too often in Stand Your Ground and self-defense cases, it is the defendant's word against a dead man's. In contrast, numerous witnesses saw the dispute at the Gate Gas Station and testified to the defendant's visible, audible anger. Perhaps most persuasive of all were the three boys who lived through the hail of gunfire. Leland, Tommie, and Tevin had all acquitted themselves as the decent, respectful young men they are. Dunn himself would never be able to see the truth of them. In one jailhouse phone call, obtained by the documentary filmmakers who were following the trial, Dunn complained to Rouer:

"When police said that these guys didn't have a record I wondered if they were just flying under the radar. Because they were bad . . . they were all gangster rappers."

Dunn's prejudices had plainly governed his decision to reach for his gun. But even though we all knew the case was fundamentally about race, we made a calculated decision not to beat that drum. Instead, during the trial, the state focused squarely on the issue of self-defense, and whether the defendant had been justified in claiming it as a cover for his actions. While we may never know the extent to which Dunn's knowledge of Stand Your Ground factored into his decision to shoot Jordan, there is no doubt he expected the law would allow him to walk away from murdering my son. In the end, it didn't matter how mouthy my teenager had been. All that mattered was Dunn's choice to reach for his gun and to continue shooting at the Durango while it was speeding away. This more than anything else revealed his true mind-set—and it wasn't fear. It was murderous rage.

At his sentencing hearing two weeks later, I walked to the front of the courtroom to offer a victim's statement. After I talked about our first days with Jordan, the prayers we had for him, the joy we took in his inquisitive, fun-filled nature, I spoke about our losses—the milestones we wouldn't ever get to see: his high school graduation, college, his marriage, grandchildren.

I paused then, not sure if I could say the next words I had written. Despite all I had lost, the Lord has asked me, as I knelt in St. Patrick's Cathedral weeks after my son's death, to forgive his murderer. In the two years since then, I had tried to do so, though I had not entirely succeeded. But standing at the podium on the day of sentencing, I searched inside myself and realized that I had in fact released my son's killer to God's judgment. The guilty verdict had helped enormously, and now I could finally lay down the great burden of blame. Though my vision was blurred by tears, I looked my son's killer in the face as I spoke the words I had written the evening before, and which I now realized were completely true: "I choose to forgive you, Mr. Dunn, for taking my son's life. I choose to release the seeds of bitterness and anger that would not honor my son's life. I choose to walk in the freedom of knowing God's justice has been served . . . I pray that God has mercy on your soul."

Ron was not nearly so magnanimous in his statement. In fact, he stated very clearly that he had *not* forgiven his son's murderer, and God would have to deal with him on that. "I haven't enough space on this paper or time in my life to tell you the feelings in my mind and my body," Ron said. "All I can say is the old Ron Davis, for all intents and purposes, died that night with Jordan. I held my son in the hospital and kissed him goodbye. You see, I gave him the first kiss when he came into this world, and I could never imagine giving him his last kiss." He broke down then, and walked over to the person in the courtroom who understood most deeply what he was feeling. The father of my child embraced me, weeping.

Then it was time for Judge Healey to pronounce the sentence. "Mr. Dunn, this tragedy could have and should have been avoided," he began. "You hear people talk about and debate their rights under Stand Your Ground and there is such a huge misunderstanding among the general public about that term. Self-defense, justifiable homicide, and excusable homicide are very complicated legal doctrines and laws, and while that debate will, I'm sure, continue, we should remember there is nothing wrong with retreating or de-escalating a situation."

With that, the judge sentenced Michael Dunn to life in prison without possibility of parole, to be served consecutively with thirty-year sentences for each of the attempted murder charges, and fifteen years for shooting into an occupied vehicle, to be served concurrently. "To lose a child is a parent's worst nightmare," Judge Healey said, "and Mr. Dunn your life is effectively over."

Dunn did make an obligatory apology in the courtroom, but in it, he maintained that his shooting of Jordan had been justified. "I was in fear of my life and did what I thought I had to do," he said. At no point did he take responsibility for committing the senseless murder of an unarmed teen. Indeed, his response to the verdict, as expressed in yet another jailhouse phone call to Rouer, was unrepentant. "It's absurd," he told his fiancée. "Everything is fucking absurd. I'm the fucking victim here. It's a hundred percent on Jordan, a hundred percent. I don't even take a half a percent. He made that happen. You know, maybe he would have killed somebody if it hadn't been for me."

I might never have known about Dunn's jailhouse rants if it hadn't been for the documentary film crew following Ron and me through the two trials. The film, written and directed by Marc Silver and ultimately titled *3½ Minutes, Ten Bullets*, would go on to win the Special Jury Prize for Social Impact at the Sundance Film Festival and be shortlisted for an Academy Award. And on November 23, 2015, the third anniversary of Jordan's death, it would premiere on HBO. As we'd hoped, the documentary inspired conversations within families, as well as in churches, schools, and workplaces about implicit bias, institutionalized racism, and gun violence. Ron and I had agreed to expose our lives to the filmmakers' camera as a way to elevate the national consciousness around these issues and to encourage people of all walks to join hands and hearts to transform our world.

Critics praised the film widely, while Ron and I appreciated that it gave the world a sense of the funny and well-loved son and friend Jordan had been. The filmmakers had also recorded the public's outcry after the first trial, when it had seemed that Dunn might get away with the murder of an unarmed black boy, especially so soon after Zimmerman was acquitted. But Jordan's case had a different ending. By documenting our pursuit of justice for Jordan, and making his short life and senseless death more widely known, the film makes it harder for people to say, this has nothing to do with me. It brings home that racism and gun violence are national crosses we all must bear, because none of us knows whose house will be the next one visited.

There is a moment in *3½ Minutes*, after the jury in the first trial deadlocked on the first-degree murder charge, when protesters outside the Duval County courthouse pour onto the nighttime streets of Jacksonville in an unplanned protest. The camera zooms in on an older black man in the crowd, his eyes weary. He is dressed in a brown suit and a fedora like my father used to wear. Looking into his creased face, I thought of how long men like him had been out here in these streets, marching for our common humanity, decade after decade, and so little had changed.

Now, however, we had posted one small victory on the civil rights battlefield. We had pushed back against gun violence and cried out that a black boy's life has value. And in the state of Florida, where the Stand Your Ground doctrine had been inaugurated, an almost all-white jury had delivered on the American promise of justice for all.

Several months later, Ron and I received word from State Attorney Angela Corey that several jurors from the second trial wanted to speak with us. Right after the trial, we had mentioned to Corey our wish to thank the jurors personally, so when they reached out to her, she agreed to set up a meeting in a conference room at her office.

Ron, Carolina, and I sat down with six of the jurors—three white men, one white woman, one black woman, and one black man. The jury foreman was there, a young man with long blond hair and wire-rimmed glasses, whose name was Wayne Davis. He not only shared Jordan's last name, but also his birthday. Wayne told us that before the trial began, before they even knew what the case was going to be about, the jurors had clasped hands in the jury room and prayed. "We asked for wisdom to render a verdict that was the truth," he said, "because we always knew there would be two sides to the story. We had to figure out what was the truth, who was telling the truth, and where that truth lies. And we all took it very, very seriously."

Our jurors not only prayed before the trial, they also prayed before they deliberated, and they prayed again after they had all agreed on the verdict. But what touched me most of all was that they also prayed for us. They really did believe the evidence showed our boys to be innocent, and they wanted us to know they were continuing to pray for us to find peace in the midst of such a devastating loss. It was clear to them that Jordan had been a good kid, and they wanted to express their condolences.

I left that meeting with the six jurors full of wonder at the hand of the Lord. Only God could have put together that devout group of people, who petitioned him at every step to help them reach a verdict that was just. I could hardly believe that while I had been earnestly praying over the outcome, the jurors had been praying, too.

When people ask me now what made the difference, I could cite all the facts of the case we had going for us, and the strategic decisions the state made about how to present the evidence. But there is one answer that rings truer than all the others for me: God was in that courtroom, and in that jury room. God had stirred our twelve jurors' hearts, and now he was stirring my own heart to become a crusader in his cause. It was as if he were saying to me: *I have ensured earthly justice for my beloved child, Jordan. I have carried you across the water. And now I need you to step out of the boat and help me to care for the rest of my beloved children.*

CHAPTER 18

God, the Protector

I WAS ON A PLANE, heading back to Atlanta after a speaking appearance in Washington, DC, when I caught wind of the sit-in. At noon that Wednesday, House Democrats had marched onto the congressional floor waving posters and chanting the names of gun victims. Led by longtime civil rights activist John Lewis of Georgia, they demanded that Speaker Paul Ryan call for a vote on two measures: the first to bar the sale of firearms to people on the FBI's no-fly list, and the second aimed at tightening loopholes in background checks on gun purchases.

To most of America, both were commonsense responses to the massacre that had unfolded in a gay nightclub in Orlando, Florida, less than two weeks before. On June 12, 2016, Omar Mateen, a local man who had previously ranted against LGBTQ people, opened fire inside Pulse nightclub, killing forty-nine and wounding fifty-eight more. The shooter, who died in the ensuing police standoff, had once been on the FBI's terror watch list, yet he'd managed to legally acquire the semiautomatic weapons used in what was, up to then, the deadliest mass shooting in modern US history.

The catalogue of such tragedies before—and after—Orlando is soul-crushing. Almost a year prior, a young man named Dylann Roof had been welcomed into an evening Bible study group at one of the nation's oldest black churches, the Emanuel African Methodist Episcopal Church in Charleston, South Carolina. After sitting with the prayerful group for an hour, the taciturn young man with blond hair falling into his eyes suddenly began gunning down the congregants, killing nine. Roof, it turned out, identified with white supremacist hate groups and had a felony drug charge pending against him. The felony charge should have prevented him from ever acquiring a firearm, yet he was able to walk into a gun store and purchase a Glock .45-caliber pistol and five magazines of bullets, without being flagged by the National Instant Criminal Background Check System as a drug abuser.[1]

The year that followed the Charleston church tragedy averaged more than one mass shooting per day—defined as an event in which four or more people are injured or killed by firearms. That violent record culminated in the Orlando nightclub massacre. And yet, on June 22, 2016, Paul Ryan, the Republican Speaker of the US House of Representatives, was refusing to even consider a bill that would limit the ability of people like Mateen and Roof to legally acquire guns.

With the House due to begin a weeklong recess for the Fourth of July holiday, the Democrats hoped to force a vote. "No bill, no break," they chanted as their cohorts on the other side of the aisle scurried from the chamber. The Dems continued their protest until morning, joined by most of their Senate colleagues. They live-streamed the sit-in on Twitter and Facebook, with the feeds quickly picked up by C-SPAN. Aides and staff members brought in food, pillows, blankets, and sleeping bags, as outside on the steps of the Capitol Building, a crowd gathered in support of their protest. As the Republican members of the House exited the building, hundreds of people outside the Capitol jeered, "Do your job!"

As soon as my flight landed in Atlanta, I turned right around and headed back to the nation's capital. This was my fight, too. Ever since the court proceedings that had ended with the conviction of my son's killer, I had felt an urgency to embrace more fully the advocacy work God had called me to do. I now believed that this work had been waiting for me ever since I was a young child marching alongside my parents in the civil rights movement. And I understood the call to serve in the most elemental terms: I was to help save lives.

Specifically, I was to accomplish this task by agitating tirelessly for stronger gun regulations. I was to march in the streets and stand in rooms and on stages across the country, talking to people about the dangers of bad gun laws like Stand Your Ground. I was to open their eyes to loopholes in background check laws and the dangers of assault weapons, and encourage people of faith to put their trust in God's protection, rather than in their sidearm. The latter stance would bring me into direct contact with white Christian evangelicals, who despite being fervently pro-life when it came to a woman's right to choose, tended to view any attempt to regulate firearms—which claim thirty-three thousand American lives each year—as trampling on their fundamental freedoms.

When peace activist Abigail Disney decided to make a film exploring the riddle of America's Christian pro-life community being also unabashedly pro-gun, Rev. Rob Schenck was a natural choice as her subject. Rob, an ordained evangelical minister, is pro-life in all senses of the word, having fought in the trenches of the right-to-life movement since the Supreme Court upheld a woman's right to choose to terminate her pregnancy in 1973. But in 1992, after the good reverend led a citywide rally to shut down abortion clinics in Buffalo, New York, a lone gunman shot and killed Dr. Barnett Slepian, a physician connected to one of the clinics. The doctor's family laid blame for the murder squarely at the minister's feet, insisting that his pro-life evangelizing had inflamed the gunman. Deeply disturbed by the accusation, Rob was plunged into a moral crisis by the possibility that he'd contributed to the death of another human being. From that day on, he began to grapple with a theological conundrum: Could one truly be pro-life and yet also be pro-gun?

Abigail convinced Rob to allow her to delve into the question with him through the lens of his Christian faith. As a feminist, she also sought a woman on the front lines of gun-violence prevention who might offer an additional perspective. I became that woman, allowing the filmmakers to record my trajectory into activism after losing Jordan. *The Armor of Light*, an Emmy Award–winning film, follows Rob Schenck and me as we engage in theological discussions about God and guns.

The roots of the seemingly incongruous alliance between Christian evangelicalism and pro-gun ardor run deep in our nation's history. "The story behind evangelicals and guns begins at the inception of our American republic," Rob explains. He notes that "plenty of early American Presbyterians, Baptists, and others took up arms not only in the war against the British, but later as settlers in America's western expansion. Various brands of evangelicalism took root in the lonely frontier, and a gun was present in these settlers' everyday lives for hunting and defense." Since that time, he says, an ideological devotion to gun rights has been a part of the evangelical DNA.[2]

To justify the prevalence of shockingly well-armed white militias on the American landscape, modern-day evangelical leaders cite the need to defend against government incursions that threaten their way of life. According to Rob Schenck: "There is a serious breakdown of trust between the evangelical Christian community and the federal government—a phenomenon that may be thanks in large part to the historical prevalence of southern evangelicalism and the legacy of the Civil War. This tension has been exacerbated in recent years by a rack of executive, legislative, and judicial actions seen as hostile to Bible-believing Christians."[3]

It's worth noting that Christian evangelicals see no contradiction between owning a weapon, or even an armory of weapons, and being pro-life. Certainly there is a biblical case to be made for self-defense. In Corinthians 6:19–20, God explicitly asks us to hold life sacred: "Do you not know that your bodies are temples of the Holy Spirit, who is in you, whom you have received from God? You are not your own; you were bought at a price. Therefore honor God with your bodies."

Evangelical ministers further insist that not only are we to care for and protect our own bodies, we also have a responsibility to guard the lives of others who may be endangered. As Psalm 82:4 commands: "Rescue the weak and needy; Deliver them from the hand of the wicked." Passages like these are the basis of evangelicals' assertion that the Bible ordains our right to bear arms for the defense of ourselves and our community. Indeed, the core tenets of biblical teachings are love and justice, and pro–Second Amendment Christians insist that justice is more easily assured with a weapon in the gun rack. But with NRATV subversively painting "the wicked" in the most culturally divisive terms, and the nation's gun laws blatantly unequal in the way they are applied, one has to ask: Who gets to decide when the taking of a life is just?

A lonely, bitter, or deranged soul walks into a school or movie theater and mows down multitudes with semiautomatic weaponry. Gangs exact revenge in neighborhoods rife with guns. A cop in Ferguson, Missouri, shoots an unarmed black teenager who had his hands in the air, who was doing nothing more than jaywalking. None of this is biblically ordained. Nowhere do the scriptures suggest that a person who does not hold sacred *every* human life should possess the means to commit murder—and this is why we must better regulate just who should be able to acquire firearms. We need laws that will allow us to assess who can be a faithful steward of the fearsome power of a gun.

We must remember that, despite the claim of the National Rifle Association and many in the evangelical vanguard that God *wants* us to bear arms, the Bible is clear: ownership of weapons for self-defense, while *permitted* by God, is not *required* by God. Indeed, Christ's peaceful surrender to his arrest in the Garden of Gethsemane, even though his disciples stood ready with swords to defend him, is powerful testimony that the Lord would rather we lay down our own life than fatally spill the blood of another. As 1 Samuel 17:47 says: "All those gathered here will know that it is not by sword or spear that the Lord saves; for the battle is the Lord's."

———

In modern-day America, if we are ever to reach consensus on gun laws that will keep all our families safe, reform advocates must find a way to build bridges to pro–Second Amendment Christian evangelicals, convinced as they are of their God-given right to bear arms. With this goal in mind, I have engaged in hundreds of conversations with white evangelicals about the moral instruction of Jesus Christ and how it might inform our beliefs and behavior around guns. Sometimes, we are able to agree that carrying a concealed weapon means we walk through the world feeling the lethal power of the gun on our hip more than the supremacy of God in our hearts. It also means we are willing to take a human life at a moment's notice, for fear we will not be protected. This is the antithesis of the Christ gospel that entreats us to love our neighbor as ourselves, even when we feel endangered, even at the expense of our own lives.

As Chris Williams, a Christian contributor to Patheos, an online journal of religious thought, writes: "We don't fear for our lives—we know death brings us to Christ and we know we're protected by the sovereignty of God. And we don't fear the other. We love them. We pray for them. We show them Christ, even if that means we lay down our right to take their lives."[4]

In other words, God is our ultimate protector, and if we truly believe in his divine power and authority, we can liberate ourselves from the fear that our fellow citizen, though different from us, might threaten our very existence. This is, of course, a deeply pacifist perspective, a submission of self that is antithetical to the American way. And yet it is Christ's way; it is the promise that true followers of Jesus make when they commit their lives to the teachings of the Gospel.

That said, most gun safety activists take no issue with owning firearms for hunting or recreation, and would never suggest that people abandon the defense of themselves and their families. But we don't need arsenals of semiautomatic weapons to do that. We don't need gun rooms stocked with assault rifles and high-capacity magazines. More to the point, we will not be prevented from protecting our families by strengthening current gun laws—requiring universal background checks with no backdoor workarounds for gun shows and private sales; sensible limits on concealed and open carry in public spheres; and statutes that diminish the likelihood of guns being acquired by domestic abusers, violent offenders, and the mentally ill.

Despite the NRA's resistance to any form of oversight, more than 90 percent of Americans *want* tighter gun regulations. A majority of God-fearing, law-abiding gun owners agree that their ability to safeguard loved ones would be enhanced by such laws, rather than undermined. Even our legislators recognize that the presence of guns in a public context only makes us less safe—why else would Congress explicitly ban firearms in its chambers and on its legislative floors. And yet Congress refuses to restrict these deadly weapons in other public spaces. Many states now allow guns in stores, bars, coffeehouses, public parks, concert venues, and even on college campuses. There has been a "guns everywhere" push on the part of the gun lobby to make concealed carry laws in one state reciprocal to all states. In effect, Concealed Carry Reciprocity, also known as CCR, would make the weakest state gun regulations the law of the land, amplifying the potential for violence. The reckless, shoot-first mentality so widely exhibited in Stand Your Ground states further compounds the problem.

While gun safety advocates have been able to convince a growing number of federal and state legislators of this point, too often the fever pitch of the NRA's messaging—along with the promise of future election campaign dollars—drowns out our voices. This unresponsiveness to appeals for commonsense gun regulations also occurs in conversations with a certain segment of evangelicals, those whose identification with the religious right is more a declaration of political affiliation and white nationalist sentiment than it is of the biblical observance of their faith. Often, in my efforts to connect with these "political evangelicals," I am confronted with parroted Second Amendment rhetoric that I recognize as the talking points of the gun lobby.

In such instances, I fall back on objective research. I might share, for example, that while many of us have bought into the fiction that arming ourselves will keep us from becoming victims, study after study reveals the NRA mantra of "more guns, less crime" to be utterly and demonstrably false. Two-thirds of Americans believe that having a gun in the home makes them safer, yet research shows that the higher the rate of gun ownership in a state, the higher the rate of violent crimes.[5]

Predictably, gun lobbyists argue that high crime rates have led to people arming themselves, and not the other way around. The study "Firearm Ownership and Violent Crime in the U.S." definitively counters that claim, showing that the escalation of violent crime in high gun-owning states *followed* the rise in gun ownership by one to two years. "Our findings refute the argument that gun ownership deters strangers from committing homicide," said Boston University's Dr. Michael Siegel, who led the research team. "Instead, these findings suggest that gun ownership actually increases the risk of violent death."[6]

Think about it. If owning and carrying guns really kept us from harm, our nation would be the safest one on earth, given that there are currently some three hundred million firearms in circulation. Yet compared to twenty-two other high-income nations (including Australia, Canada, Germany, Japan, England, and France), Americans are twenty-five times more likely to die in gun homicides.[7] Even more troubling, in America a gun in the home is far more likely to be used in an attempted or successful suicide, criminal assault or murder, or accidental shooting than it is to be used for self-defense. In fact, Everytown for Gun Safety reports that for every instance a gun kills someone in a legal intervention, guns are used forty-five times in a suicide, twenty-five times in a homicide, and up to four times in an unintentional shooting that results in death.[8] And here's another staggering fact: suicide attempts using a firearm succeed 90 percent of the time, while suicide attempts using other means *fail* 90 percent of the time.[9]

What all this adds up to is that a frightening number of guns fall into the hands of people who are not responsible custodians of such deadly firepower. Unfortunately, legislators in Congress aren't acting to protect us. Too many of them have been bought by the NRA, which makes it crucial for organizations like Everytown and Moms Demand Action to identify and support candidates who are not beholden to gun lobby money, and who, once elected, will be free to vote with their common sense and conscience. Responsible public officials know that the fight for gun safety has never been about infringing on Americans' right to acquire and use firearms. We simply want to make sure that, despite the gun lobby's rhetoric of hate and fear, everyone who acquires a firearm will be a good steward of that weapon, and that the laws by which we as a nation abide will support that utterly pro-life objective.

CHAPTER 19

Hope Dealers

IN MY EXPERIENCE, WHITE EVANGELICAL audiences tend to harbor a deep strain of racial prejudice, one that my very presence in their midst tends to expose. I never shrink from engaging this racial antipathy. I remain optimistic that we can find a common cause in the fight for gun safety. We have only to begin listening to one another to bridge the cultural and spiritual divide in our country.

Two political scientists at the University of Illinois at Chicago sought to explain the source of white resentment against people of color and the ways in which it fuels white resistance to regulating firearms. The researchers, Drs. Alexandra Filinara and Noah Kaplan, drew on research from across academic disciplines for their study "Racial Resentment and Whites' Gun Policy Preferences in Contemporary America." They found that "the language of individual freedom used by the gun rights movement utilizes the same racially meaningful tropes as the rhetoric of the white resistance to black civil rights that developed after WWII and into the 1970s. This indicates that the gun rights narrative is color-coded and evocative of racial resentment."[1]

Of course, I have always known this. One cannot walk through this country in black skin and not sense the reflexive resistance many whites feel toward any agenda they believe is for the greater good of an ethnic "other." The National Rifle Association also understands this, and they have exploited it to deepen racial divisions at every turn.

The shooting of Philando Castile is a flagrant and heartrending example. Castile was a nutrition services supervisor for a public school in St. Paul, Minnesota. A temperate soul who was well loved by students, Castile had memorized the food allergies of some five hundred of the children. And yet, outside of that place where he was known, he had been pulled over by area police forty-nine times, sometimes for minor traffic infractions, and sometimes for no reason at all—a hazard known among African Americans as "driving while black."

On July 6, 2016, Castile was driving in a St. Paul suburb with his girlfriend beside him in the front passenger seat and her four-year-old daughter riding in the back of the white Oldsmobile. Police stopped Castile's car and asked to see his ID. They said he had a broken taillight. They didn't mention that, in a classic case of mistaken identity, another officer had radioed them saying Castile and his girlfriend "look like people that were involved in a robbery. The driver looks more like one of our suspects, just because of the wide-set nose."[2]

Officer Jeronimo Yanez approached Castile's window and requested to see his driver's license and proof of insurance. As Castile handed him the insurance card, he politely informed the officer that he had a firearm in the car and a permit to carry it. He then explained that he was reaching for his license as Yanez had asked him to do. Less than a minute later, Castile was bleeding to death in the front seat of his car, shot five times by Yanez at close range, twice through the heart. The police dash cam caught the whole episode, while Castile's terrified girlfriend streamed the immediate aftermath of the shooting live on Facebook. By the next afternoon 2.5 million people had watched a black man shot to death for legally exercising his Second Amendment right to bear arms. And the NRA said nothing.

When the cop who shot Castile was acquitted of all charges a year later, the NRA still hadn't issued any statement in support of a gun owner with a legal permit to carry, and who had done everything by the book.

In another telling incident, John Crawford III, a twenty-two-year-old African American man, was shot dead by cops in the sporting goods section of a Beavercreek, Ohio, Walmart. On August 5, 2014, Crawford, the father of two sons, picked up a BB gun from the store's open shelf. Suddenly cops were bearing down on him, weapons drawn. "It's a toy! It's a toy!" Crawford cried, as bullets flew at him. I'm fairly sure that all the cops saw as they squeezed the trigger was the scary construct of a black criminal that too many law-enforcement officers carry in their heads. But why did the NRA fail to issue a statement defending Crawford? Why did they neglect to point out that he was holding a BB gun in the store that sold it, and that even if the gun had been real, the state's open carry laws should have shielded this innocent shopper from deadly police action?

I could go on, citing example after example of the NRA's double standard when it comes to black gun owners. But you already know I'm not making this up. *Boston Globe* columnist Michael A. Cohen told the glaring truth when he asserted: "Let's be honest, for many of those dedicated NRA gun owners, the threat of crime and of assault has a black face. For years, the NRA has cultivated and deepened that particular prejudice. Indeed, the original impetus for new gun laws in the 1960s was the push by radical black groups for African Americans to arm themselves in self-defense. Perversely, a similar push today might be the only effective path to stronger gun control laws in America.

"Philando Castile might have been a legal gun owner," Cohen

concluded, "but as is so often the case in America, race trumps all. While it's very difficult to disconnect his death from race, it's even harder to find any other explanation for the disconcerting silence of the nation's most vocal advocates for gun ownership."[3]

Every senseless gun death brings me right back to Jordan, reminding me why I do this work, advocating for commonsense gun laws that the NRA's leadership thwarts ruthlessly. It was not lost on me that in the cases of Philando Castile and John Crawford III the gun lobby and I should have been on the same side: the Second Amendment rights of law-abiding citizens had been infringed upon, yet from the NRA leadership, we heard crickets.

Contrast this with the NRA's vociferous calls for more guns in schools after twenty children and six educators died at Sandy Hook. And after the Orlando nightclub shooting, they were quick to trot out the tired old standby that "the only way to stop a bad man with a gun is a good man with a gun." Never mind the fact that scores of citizens brandishing firearms in an active shooter situation would only confuse law enforcement as to exactly who the good and bad men were. And of course, the risk of unintended shooting deaths would rise exponentially. Nevertheless, the NRA nakedly uses such tragedies to push their talking points, stoke fear, and gin up gun sales.

Yet every day we are gaining ground. "When you look at what's happening in statehouses across the country, the gun safety movement is winning in state after state, even in this challenging political environment," says Shannon Watts, founder of Moms Demand Action for Gun Sense in America. "Volunteers and gun violence survivors have become the counterweight to the gun lobby. [We are] defeating dangerous proposals like permitless carry and guns in schools, and helping to pass life-saving measures to keep guns out of the hands of domestic abusers."[4]

Through the efforts of this committed army of activists, the campaign for gun reform has posted significant victories: In the past five years, for example, lawmakers in twenty-five states have engaged in a bipartisan effort to keep guns from being acquired by domestic abusers. In 2017 alone, despite the presence of an NRA-backed president in the White House, eight states passed this legislation: Louisiana, Maryland, Nevada, New Jersey, North Dakota, Rhode Island, Tennessee, and Utah.[5]

In addition, the gun violence prevention movement has managed to defeat numerous bills designed to advance the NRA's "guns everywhere" drive. Targeted advocacy by Moms Demand Action chapters nationwide, along with aggressive social media outreach to educate the public, led to the overwhelming rejection of legislation that would have allowed people to carry concealed, loaded firearms without a permit. In twenty of the twenty-two states where such bills were introduced, the proposals were defeated. Even South Dakota's governor, an NRA member, vetoed the bill.[6]

Similarly, legislation to allow guns on college campuses failed in fourteen of the sixteen states where it was introduced, and an NRA priority bill to allow firearms in K–12 schools was prevented in all but one of the eighteen states where it was pushed. Meanwhile, efforts to repeal background check laws in Iowa and Nebraska were rejected in large part because Moms Demand Action volunteers called, wrote, emailed, and met with legislators in a concerted way, urging them to block such a disastrous rolling back of gun safety regulations.[7]

Even in the case of Stand Your Ground, the NRA's signature legislative issue, gun violence prevention advocates have seen progress. Despite the law still being on the books in twenty-four states as of this writing, several state legislative bodies have introduced bills that would make the application of the law more fair, including repealing grants of immunity from civil or criminal action for those who invoke the doctrine after using deadly force, and bolstering the "duty to retreat" when such retreat might lead to the preservation of life.[8]

All these wins keep us going, while the inevitable setbacks only force us to dig deeper, to find new and innovative ways to counter the gun lobby's tricky agenda by winning hearts and minds on both sides of America's vast cultural chasm.

———

Sometimes, on a particularly hard day, I will pull out a black T-shirt sent to me by Pastor Michael McBride after the first jury deadlocked on the conviction of our son's killer. Pastor Mike is the national director of urban strategies and Live Free campaign for the PICO National Network, which brings together hundreds of faith congregations to tackle gun violence and mass incarceration of youth of color. Pastor Mike understood the need for us to keep in sight why we fight, and so he gifted Ron and me with T-shirts on which the words "HOPE DEALERS" appeared in large block letters on the front.

Whenever I wear that T-shirt now, it reminds me that I am working to give those who are disproportionately affected by gun violence an enduring sense of hope. We want people to see that we are in the midst of an awakening. Across the country, Black Lives Matter groups are mobilizing; students outraged by the regularity of school shootings are marching for their lives; mayors are organizing to pass stricter laws; and mothers are galvanizing their communities to run and elect officials willing to challenge the political status quo.

Our churches, too, have a role to play in bringing peace to our world. African American theologians are well placed to implement life-saving initiatives in communities fractured by poverty, where gangs and guns proliferate and bullets too often settle conflicts. But preachers must take their message from the pulpit to the street, walking and talking with their neighbors, listening to their troubles, and helping them find alternatives to violence in their lives. Preachers must help their flock believe from the depths of their souls that God's love is the ultimate protection, and that their lives are deeply valued. In a more practical vein, they must help their congregations understand which electoral candidates have their interests at heart, and then get their congregants to the polls.

Churches can also create safe spaces for the community, where children can do homework after school, the unemployed can get help finding jobs, trauma victims can find counseling, and ex-cons can tap into a network of support that will keep them from falling back into crime. As Pastor Mike, the ultimate hope dealer, explains, "When interventions are grounded in love, care, opportunity, and healing—with consequences for those who continue to engage in destructive behaviors—powerful transformation and change happens, and folks actually stop engaging in that kind of violence. The challenge is to address the local manifestations of the problem, realizing that it does not require racial profiling, aggressive policing, mass incarceration, and other over-policing remedies. They are not necessary, because the perpetrators, and the victims, are all so focused and narrowly networked that we can intervene with them with strategic and targeted approaches."[9]

One very pointed and effective strategy is for pastors to take the lead in building bridges between law enforcement and their communities. In Harlem, New York, for example, one Episcopal minister makes a point of walking alongside police officers on the beat. As they walk, they stop and talk to people in the neighborhood, they exchange names and stories, they share pride in their children, the worries that keep them up at night, hopes for the future. They become *known* to one another, so that the next time they meet, whether the circumstance is benevolent or challenging, they are no longer strangers. They meet now as familiars, each perhaps more willing to give the other the benefit of the doubt. The result might well be that a gun is never drawn from a holster or a pocket. Shots are never fired. Everyone goes home alive.

In the ceaseless struggle to prevent gun violence, these kinds of efforts will have to be sustained. When one considers how long our nation has grappled with its present culture of racial resentment and fear, it becomes clear these attitudes will not be dismantled overnight. I confess that, until an angry white man murdered my child, I had believed our country to be more "post-racial" than it actually ever was. I had lived in a bubble of privilege, able to travel the world with my son and give him a good life. Ron and I had done well enough financially to provide for all of Jordan's needs, and many of his wants. Our comforts had blinded me to the true depths of racism in this country. But Jordan's death opened my eyes. In fighting to get justice for him, Stand Your Ground became emblematic of the ways in which justice had been systematically denied to people of color in this country for eons.

Looking back now, I'm shocked at my naiveté. Growing up in the civil rights movement, traveling to marches and protest rallies with my parents, I should have known better. I even have pictures of my father standing with President Lyndon B. Johnson as he signed the Civil Rights Act. Since then, my own awakening has been hard-won, and the price I was forced to pay for it could not have been more extreme. It is why I feel such a charge now to help save lives, and why I will never allow the hope for a more equitable future to grow cold in my heart.

I might never see the fruit of the seeds I am sowing now, just as my parents did not live to see the great expression of their work in the election of a black man as president. But future generations will harvest this crop, and be nourished to continue the struggle. Still, it astounds me to realize that fifty years later, I'm not done fighting the battles Daddy raised me to fight. Lucien Holman was a complicated figure in my life, but he showed me what it means to give unwavering commitment to a cause, even one that might outlast you. Daddy taught me to believe in the seeds of hope we press into the earth. He showed me how to be a hope dealer.

CHAPTER 20

Say Their Names

AS I'D LANGUISHED IN A wilderness of grief after Jordan died, God had said to me, *I will take you places you have never been, for the people must see my face.* And in July 2016, God placed me, along with eight other African American mothers who had lost their children to violence, on the Democratic National Convention stage. We had been introduced to the world as the Mothers of the Movement, nine women with red roses pinned over our hearts to symbolize the blood of our children. Thirty-two million people would hear us testify that night and I wanted to get it right. More than anything, I wanted people to know that we could all work together to bring about change; to stop our sons and daughters from being shot dead in the streets; to create a "more perfect union" in which the sanctity of every person's life could be preserved.

"You don't stop being a mom when your child dies," I told the delegates when it was my turn at the microphone. "You don't stop being a parent when your child dies. I am still Jordan Davis's mother. His life ended the day he was shot and killed for playing loud music, but my job as his mother didn't. I still wake up every day thinking about how to parent him, how to protect him and his legacy, how to ensure that his death doesn't overshadow his life." My fight to repeal dangerous gun laws like Stand Your Ground, I explained, was my way of parenting Jordan now.

"We're going to keep telling our children's stories," I added, feeling the brimming emotion of the other mothers beside me on that stage. "And we're urging you to say their names. We're going to keep building a future where police officers and communities of color work together in mutual respect to keep children like Jordan safe."

I'd met many of the mothers on that stage before that night, but now it struck me how powerful we could be as a group. In the months that followed, we appeared together at events throughout the country, speaking at churches, rallies, and town halls, urging people to get out and vote in the coming presidential election. Of the original twelve mothers, I found myself most often in the company of a core group of six women.

Sybrina Fulton, mother of Trayvon Martin, was the most widely recognized. With her ex-husband, Tracy Martin, she had become a lightning rod for a new civil rights movement that was now so established that we knew it by its acronym, BLM. I called Sybrina "The Stateswoman." She was unfailingly calm and dignified, a quiet and forceful leader.

Maria Hamilton was "The Organizer," able to turn out five hundred people for a rally on a dime. I'd seen her rustle up a protest march outside a courthouse overnight, in a strange city, on the fly. She was just talented that way. Her son, Dontre Hamilton, had suffered with mental illness. At age thirty-one, he'd been shot fourteen times by Milwaukee police who found him sleeping on a park bench. He had been unarmed.

Geneva Reed-Veal was "The Evangelist," a natural preacher

woman who didn't need a teleprompter or a script to raise the Holy Ghost. When Geneva stepped up to speak, it was church. In yet another senseless tragedy, her twenty-eight-year-old daughter, Sandra Bland, had died suspiciously in police custody after a traffic stop in Waller County, Texas.

Gwen Carr's son, forty-three-year-old Eric Garner, had been choked to death by New York City police as they tried to arrest him for selling loose cigarettes. Gwen was "Mother Love," a tender-hearted soul, the gentle grandmother of the group, the one we all wanted to rally around and protect.

Cleopatra Cowley-Pendleton was "The Optimist," the one who lifted other people's spirits and put everyone at ease. Her usual cheer couldn't hide her heartbreak, though. Her fifteen-year-old daughter Hadiya Pendleton, an honor student, had been shot by a stray bullet in a Chicago park on the day after she marched with her high school band at Obama's second inauguration.

As for me, I was dubbed "The Politician," the one most likely to be found in statehouses rattling off talking points and lobbying for gun law reform. The six of us, and many others who joined us from time to time, committed ourselves to spreading the message that, while it was too late to save our own children, voters could exercise their power at the polls to save their own.

In the months leading up to the November 2016 election, I made a heavy emotional investment in the promise of one candidate to transform the nation's gun culture, and I was impatient to have the race decided. The night before the momentous vote, unable to sleep, I drove to my local mall, wanting to be out among people. Inside one store, I noticed a young African American man. He reminded me slightly of Tommie Stornes, who had been driving the red Dodge Durango the night Jordan was killed, which may be why he caught my eye. He was wiry in build, with neat dreadlocks framing a lean, handsome face. His jeans rode low on his hips, and his sneaker game was on point. The thought occurred to me that he was exactly the sort of young man who might be unfairly profiled by law enforcement or white vigilantes who couldn't see past their unconscious or overt biases. That made me sad. As if sensing my attention, the young man looked over at me, nodded politely, and smiled.

"Did you vote early?" I asked him cheerfully.

He shook his head. "No, ma'am."

"That's okay," I said, "just make sure you vote tomorrow."

His response stopped me in my tracks.

"I'm not voting," he said, his beautiful young face cynical. "I'm going to let America hang itself."

I could not get this young man out of my mind as voters delivered a candidate endorsed by the National Rifle Association to the White House one night later. I felt the loss viscerally, as if I had personally failed to convey the depth of the moral wounding that had led to my activism. We who had lost sons and daughters to police and vigilante violence had felt a great sense of purpose as we canvassed the nation. We had sermonized to our communities about our worth and rights as Americans, and our ability to decisively influence this critical race. Yet despite the miles we traveled, many of our own people did not hear our plea. Our turnout in 2016 was 7 percentage points lower than four years before, a margin that cost us dearly. I wanted to say to black America: *Beloveds, why did you not listen to the urgency in our voices as we begged you to uphold the legacy our ancestors gave their lives to secure? Did you not recognize your own power?*

I recalled how, on the eve of the election, I had spoken urgently to the young man in that Atlanta mall. "You cannot afford *not* to vote," I had told him. "If you let America hang itself, the noose will be around your neck and mine." I tried to explain that he would be handing the government a mandate to double down on institutionalized racism, and to literally and symbolically erase black and brown bodies like his own.

The young man only shook his head, mumbled, "Yes, ma'am" politely, and walked away. I do not believe he voted.

Today, I want to say to that same young man—and to *all* of America—that we can still do our part to prevent our nation from hanging itself. We must all stand our ground. While I fully supported the loud, peaceful protests that took over the streets in the days following the election, we now have to do more than rally. We must establish clear-eyed strategies to combat the extremism of the nation's gun lobby, so that no more of our children will die in vain.

The need for Americans from all walks to join together is critical now, and indeed, the coalition around gun safety seems to be broadening. We have reached a turning point in our nation's consciousness, the tragic result of a holocaust of mass shootings unleashed by deranged individuals who should never have been able to acquire firearms. The Las Vegas massacre on October 1, 2017, was only the latest high-water mark of death, with fifty-eight concert-goers murdered in an open field by a man firing fully automated weapons of war from the thirty-second floor of a nearby hotel.

On Valentine's Day of 2018, the trauma happened again. At Marjory Stoneman Douglas High School in Parkland, Florida, a disturbed nineteen-year-old walked into the building, set off the fire alarms to lure students into the hallways, and opened fire with an AR-15 semiautomatic rifle on which he had carved a swastika. Seventeen students and teachers were massacred in what became the eighteenth school shooting in a year that was not yet two months old.

Something shifted that day in Parkland. Heartbroken, angry, and ignited, student survivors swarmed the national news, excoriating the gun lobby and pointing out that a teen who'd declared on YouTube his intention to become a school shooter should never have been able to purchase an AR-15. Under the banner #NeverAgain, busloads of young people from across Florida poured into the state house in Tallahassee, insisting on an assault rifle ban and stronger background check laws. Masterfully deploying social media, the Parkland teens helped organize national marches against gun violence, tweeted lists of US companies doing business with the NRA, and entreated voters to make a clean sweep of politicians beholden to the gun lobby come the midterm elections.

Predictably, many politicians offered empty platitudes, but the Florida state legislature, feeling a new kind of pressure, raised the minimum age of gun buyers from eighteen to twenty-one, and instituted a three-day waiting period for background checks. And within weeks, scores of airlines, hotel chains, car rental companies, insurance giants, and media organizations staged a mass exodus from corporate partnerships with the NRA. Perhaps the most stunning evidence that a revolution in national consciousness was underway was the appearance online of videos showing gun owners smashing their assault rifles in solidarity with the students.

I cheered our young people's courage, and was inspired anew by their bedrock belief in the power of a collective to bring about change. Again and again, history has shown that when students become activated for a cause—from the civil rights movement to Black Lives Matter to #NeverAgain—the landscape is permanently transformed. Even so, we cannot underestimate the chilling calculation of the NRA's leadership as they continue to stoke the forces of hate, tribalism, and fear. As the Parkland survivors so deeply understand, we dare not fail to exercise the power of our vote.

The man who moved into the White House on inauguration day 2017 was deep in the pocket of the gun lobby, which had poured an unprecedented $30.3 million into his campaign chest.[1] The promised erosion of gun regulations began at once. In my home state of Georgia, for example, legislators passed a measure allowing college students to carry concealed firearms on public campuses, an appalling idea given the devastating school shootings our nation has endured. Congress also repealed a law aimed at preventing guns from being acquired by those diagnosed with a mental illness, and as I write this, House Republicans are preparing to lift restrictions on gun silencers, making it easier for shooters to kill without being detected, and harder for law enforcement to figure out exactly where gunfire is coming from. Unrestricted silencers will only increase the body count—while assuring a whole new profit stream for the gun industry, which is of course the point.

I have come to realize that for the gun lobby, issues of race, politics, and faith are exploited only as they serve the overarching profit motive. Capitalism is the true driver of gun violence in America. With full understanding of this, I have vowed that I will not rest until this truth is received in every corner, and if I manage to save just one life by my advocacy, maybe the life of the pessimistic young man at the Atlanta mall, my work will not be in vain.

This was my mind-set on the day after the presidential inauguration, when I walked with my fellow Mothers of the Movement in a massive Women's March for Human Rights in Washington, DC. By some estimates, the crowd in the nation's capital that day was one million deep, with most marchers wearing knitted pink hats with pointed corners in protest of the new president's vulgar, tape-recorded sexism. The global opposition to the new administration was so pitched that in countries as far-flung as South Africa and New Zealand, similar demonstrations were taking place. In all, domestically and around the world, there were 673 demonstrations in solidarity with women's rights and human rights that day. All were nonviolent, and all of them wildly exceeded expectations in terms of attendees.

Perhaps the energy of the inauguration day had been so heavy and murky, that to balance it, the world spontaneously chose brilliance, chose hope and optimism, chose to harness the energy of the divine feminine and all those who stand in its light. I believe we were all searching for a way to turn our dismay at the tone of the new administration into something positive and powerful. And we did.

At a certain point in the afternoon, singer Janelle Monáe called the Mothers of the Movement onto the main stage set up on the Washington Mall. One by one she introduced us, and asked us to speak our children's names. The entire world was watching as she put the microphone to my lips and commanded, "Say your son's name."

"Jordan Davis!" I yelled over the sea of pink hats and clenched fists and protest signs raised high.

"Say it again!" Monáe shouted.

"Jordan Davis!" I called, and the crowd picked up the chant.

"Jordan Davis! Jordan Davis! Jordan Davis!"

It was electrifying!

Jordan's name was on the lips of a million marchers, and in the ears of untold millions more. As his name rang out over the nation's capital, and was broadcast live on television screens all over the world, I remembered the evening Jordan told me, "Everyone will know my name."

———

Another night. Another screening. After the last frame of *The Armor of Light* faded to black, and the lights in the auditorium flickered on, a young woman with pink-tinged hair in the front row raised her hand. I was in New Haven, Connecticut, for a conversation on guns and faith. The Rev. Rob Schenck and peace activist Abigail Disney were once again with me on the panel, but the audience that night was as liberal and racially diverse as our audience in Columbia, South Carolina, a few weeks before had been conservative and white. It never failed to impress me that my advocacy could put me in front of such a wide and vivid cross-section of fellow Americans.

The moderator introduced each of the panelists then called on the young woman with the pink-tinged hair. Her question was addressed to me: "Which scripture in the Bible have you leaned most heavily on to help you move through the work that you do?" she asked. That was an easy one for me. I reached for the microphone and thanked her for the question, because it was always good to be reminded of the true frame of activism.

"My scripture," I told the young woman, and everyone else gathered, "is from Hebrews Chapter 11, verse one, and it is this: 'Now faith is the substance of things hoped for, the evidence of things not seen.' I live that verse every day because advocacy of any sort is not about what we can perceive with our natural eyes. It's about the seeds that we're planting, and the faith we hold on to that the work we do quickens what is happening in the spiritual realm, which in turn affects hearts and minds here."

I could have said more. I could have told that young woman that all my life I had prayed that God would use Jordan and me for his great purpose—that was my most impassioned prayer. And my Heavenly Father had answered that prayer a hundredfold. I could see it clearly now: I had received exactly what I had asked for. God had indeed used Jordan for a worthy cause. My son had sparked a revolution inside me, rousing me from my long slumber. Don't get me wrong. I am no martyr. I would rather still have my child with me in the flesh, but if I can't have that, then I choose to believe that God is using my child to help save a nation, to help deliver his people to sanctuary on the other side of the floodwaters, and that's as much as any parent could ask.

And so, in Jordan's name, I will continue to fight the good fight, to press forward with absolute faith in the connectedness of all issues of justice, and in our connectedness to one another. I truly believe that whether we acknowledge it or not, in the end, our common humanity will save us. That is why I rise each morning with just one thought, to do God's bidding with humility. And every day there is a new request to tell Jordan's story; to testify before state legislatures about the dangers of Stand Your Ground; to appear on television as the nation continues to grapple with the crisis of gun violence; and to remind my brothers and sisters in faith that our Heavenly Father is more powerful than any sidearm.

It still pains me to think that it took my son's death for me to step out of the boat and into my purpose. I have come to accept that the ache of missing Jordan never stops. I still cry myself to sleep many nights, wishing I could see and hold him one more time. I remember praying to God one evening, on my knees, weeping. "Lord," I cried, "I miss Jordan so much. I just want to see him again, Lord. I know he's with you, but I just need to see him, to know he's okay."

It was the night before Easter, and swamped by fresh waves of grief, I fell into a restless sleep. Just before daybreak, I dreamed I was in a sun-drenched garden with my parents, Lucien and Wilma. A small child played at their feet and I recognized him as my stillborn son, Lucien. And then I saw Jordan, emerging from somewhere behind my parents, walking forward through the garden slowly. He was tall and handsome in his ROTC uniform, the navy-blue cloth almost shining. He looked older, his face was more mature, and the bristling energy that always coursed through him in life seemed stilled.

I ran to him, tears of joy on my face. "You came to visit me," I whispered. "At last." My handsome boy held out his arms, the way he used to do in life when he knew I wanted to hug him. I encircled him with my arms and rested my head against the dazzling blue of his uniform. He allowed me to hold him and talk to him for several minutes. I told him how much I would always cherish the time we'd had, and I thanked him for everything he had taught me in life and after his death. He didn't say anything, but I felt enveloped in a warm glow, and I knew it was love. After a while, Jordan placed his hands on my shoulders and gently pushed me back. He stepped away from me then, and went to stand between his grandparents, the three of them smiling across at me, the sunlight falling over them with a white brilliance as the dream misted away.

When I opened my eyes, daylight was haloing the curtains. Soon, it would be time to wake Curtis and get ready for Easter morning services, but for now, I lay perfectly still, calling back the memory of Jordan in my arms. It occurred to me that, true to the biblical story that inspired my son's name, God had ushered me across the turbulent waters to a new beginning in the Promised Land. Now my feet were planted, and all I had to do was follow the call, knowing that every moment of my life had prepared me for exactly this. In the softness of daybreak, I felt the presence of all those who had gone before me, breathing courage into me for another day.

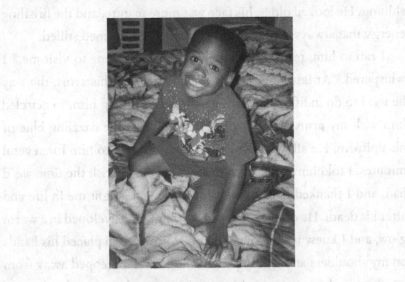

EPILOGUE

The Letter

I WAS IN MY HOME office in Marietta on the afternoon of January 18, 2017, when a letter arrived. Sunlight streamed across my desk as I slit open the plain brown envelope and unfolded the single sheet of paper inside. My eyes fell first on the black, institutional type at the top of the page: "Outreach Statement to Birth Parents." My hand flew to my mouth, and my whole body began to tremble.

Hello—
This letter is in hopes of obtaining information regarding my birth mother, father, siblings and/or relatives as closure to my hereditary and genetic uncertainty.

I am well. I was raised (well) by a stable and loving adoptive family—though there was always a subliminal disconnect as I struggled to relate to true family. True family that looked like me, talked like me and expressed themselves in the passionate ways that I do!

I realize that the disconnect was not intentional, but because of it, I have always felt the need to know about the family that completes the missing piece of my life's puzzle.

I have two beautiful children. My daughter is 21 years old and in her senior year of college. My son is 15 years old and has just begun his Freshman year of high school. We are all very small in stature, though big in heart.

Not a day of my life has gone by where I didn't think about you and I truly hope that you will consider reaching out and connecting with me. I in no way judge your decision nor place blame, so please consider this as a blessing. For you and me.

Sincerely,

Your Daughter

I read the letter again, not quite believing what I was holding in my hands. The joy that infused me as I flattened the sheet of paper to my breast was equaled only by the elation I had felt at the moment Jordan was born. So very much had been taken from me when Jordan died, but now I was astonished and humbled by all that might yet be restored.

I was not so naive as to think the road back to my daughter would be easy. There had been wrenching tragedy in my own life, and my daughter's life, too, was undoubtedly marked by the trauma of loss—of never knowing the woman who birthed her. But for me, there was also a great and abiding love, which had beat in my heart since the moment my baby girl was placed all too briefly in my arms. That is why I knew at once that I would walk through the door that had been opened to me. My daughter! And grandchildren! My granddaughter, I realized then, was the age Jordan would be had he lived, and my grandson was the age Jordan had been when he left my home and went to live with his father in Jacksonville.

I could scarcely fathom that I might once again hold a child of my body close against my heart, though I wasn't at all sure what would happen from here. In truth, I was terrified that after all these years I would be found wanting. But I would open my heart and allow our future to unfold as God willed it. Tears of pure happiness flowing down my face, I got down on my knees beside my desk, and prayed and laughed and wept and rocked, reading and re-reading that letter for a long time. At last I rose, picked up a pen, and signed the affidavit of permission that would lead me back to my living child.

APPENDIX

GET INVOLVED

Join the Campaign

Our nation needs you. The heart and soul of the campaign to prevent gun violence is the committed legion of volunteers who work passionately for the cause. Whether you already believe in our movement, or are looking to become more educated about gun issues, the following organizations, with which I am affiliated, are good places to start.

EVERYTOWN FOR GUN SAFETY

A powerful alliance of mayors, moms, survivors, faith leaders, gun owners, cops, teachers, and other ordinary Americans, Everytown fights for gun safety on numerous fronts. It funds and compiles research studies and disseminates gun violence data, while working with lawmakers to close the loopholes that allow guns to fall into dangerous hands. Founded by a network of more than 1,000 current and former mayors against illegal guns, the nonpartisan organization identifies candidates, supporters, and volunteers with the courage and conscience to face down the powerful gun lobby and stand up for policies designed to keep America safe. For more on how you can become a part of the movement, log on to everytown.org.

MOMS DEMAND ACTION FOR GUN SENSE IN AMERICA

Join forces with other moms to help find sensible solutions to the epidemic of gun violence that puts our loved ones at risk. Founded in the wake of the Sandy Hook Elementary School massacre, Moms is a nonpartisan grassroots effort to transform public opinion and mobilize communities through social media campaigns and community activism. With chapters in every state, the group has convinced many corporate and political leaders to act responsibly when it comes to firearms, and to apply pressure where it counts. To join the movement, learn about current initiatives, donate to the cause, or find an upcoming event in your city, visit momsdemandaction.org.

CHAMPION IN THE MAKING LEGACY FOUNDATION

My son, Jordan, often expressed the wish that all children be provided a quality education regardless of economic circumstance. In honor of his vision of a more perfect world, the foundation offers a summer STEM program to high school students as well as charitable assistance to graduating seniors headed to traditional colleges and universities or technical training institutions. In addition to grants of financial support, the foundation's Bridge to Millennials Program connects students with mentors who provide guidance in building life skills to black youth striving for personal and academic excellence. To donate or become a mentor, or to apply for a student scholarship, go to championinthemaking.org.

Acknowledgments

In the years since Jordan's death, I have received more love than I have room enough to contain. I want to personally thank so many people for their steadfast support and belief in me during some of the most difficult days of my life. But first, I must give honor and thanks to God for giving me Jordan and for the seventeen remarkable years I was allowed to be his mother. It has been the most important work I will ever do, and I pray I have done it well.

Thank you, Lord, for holding me in your arms when I couldn't breathe or see your light. I have come to love you in a way I never imagined possible. I truly understand my purpose now and I completely trust you with my life. Jordan is free and at peace in your divine care. I have no doubt you called him home.

To my sweet, loving husband, Curtis, whose quiet strength has been my comfort and shelter when the world overwhelmed me, you are my heart. I thank you for loving me through the good days and the hard ones, and keeping faith with me on the journey.

Thank you to my extraordinary family, whom I adore. You are the sturdy foundation beneath my feet. Lori, you loved and cared for Jordan as your own, and I am so grateful for the sunny San Diego summers he spent in your home. Dominic, thank you for sowing fatherly love and care into this "peanut head." Julian, Savannah, Levi, Anayiah, and Danielle, I am so proud of each of you, and I have loved watching you grow to be such incredible human beings. I see who Jordan could have been and what he might have done in each of you, and I know he loved you deeply. Lisa, Danielle, Linda, and Bill, I know that Daddy smiles on us from above, and I am grateful for your abiding love. His blood connects us all and I'm happy we have bonded across miles and years.

Uncle George, Cecilia, and my loving cousins, you have given so much support to Jordan and me over the years. Thank you for always making room for us when we came to town.

Ron, I think Jordan would be proud of what we have accomplished in his name. I pray you can rest in this truth as you continue to live and work on behalf of our son. I will always be thankful to you for partnering with me to bring our beautiful boy into the world. We did well.

Terri and Earl, thank you for being there for me whenever I need you, day or night, year after year. At all times, you have been my greatest allies and my best friends. I love you both dearly.

Cheryl and Steve, I can never repay you for the two-and-a-half years when you took me into your home and gave me unconditional love during those dark and painful days of fighting for Jordan and the other boys in court. Through every hearing, interview, and pretrial motion you stood by my side.

To Leland, Tommie, and Tevin, I pray for each of you often, and I am forever grateful that Jordan spent his last hours on this earth happy in your company. Thank you for your grace and perseverance through the storm. I wish you and your loved ones light-filled days from here on.

Conrad, Yvette, MeMe, Aloma, and David, I love you for covering

Jordan and me and becoming our extended family in Georgia when we felt like orphans with no blood relatives nearby to call our own. You are the village God promised me during those days when I was raising my beautiful Jordan.

To Deedra, Gwen, and my Champion in the Making family, without your dedication to Jordan's expressed wish that all children be afforded a quality education, I could never fulfill his dream. He lives on through your efforts. Over the years, I have also welcomed the love and support of my Delta Sigma Theta Sorority sisterhood.

Pastors Pam Calhoun, Artis Crum Sr., Jim Bolin, and Dr. Q, your Godly wisdom and patient guidance over the years taught me to lean on the Lord for all things. You have been the greatest spiritual mentors and teachers I have ever known.

To my Moms Demand Action for Gun Sense in America and Everytown for Gun Safety families, thank you for giving me a voice and a platform to prick the conscience of America so that someday we will all be set free from gun violence. Shannon Watts, John Feinblatt, Chris Kocher, Erika Soto-Lamb, Stephanie Stone, Ify Ike, Kirsten Moore, and Kim Russell, you will never know how much I value what I have learned from you about organizing and activism. As I have always said, I am an accidental activist, but you have charged me to fight every day for a safer America. Thank you for pushing me to broaden my vision, to expand my work, and to go where the Lord leads me to save as many lives as possible.

Abby Disney, Rob Schenck, Kathy Hughes, Stephanie Palumbo, Carolyn Hepburn, Su Patel, Julie Goldman, Bonni Cohen, Minette Nelson, David Echols, Orlando Bagwell, and Marc Silver, thank you for helping us to share Jordan's story through the creation of award-winning social impact documentaries. You helped both Ron and me to elevate Jordan's story and bring it to a nation crying out for justice and an end to gun violence. His story has become a thread woven into the history of this nation because you made it so.

To attorneys John Phillips, Angela Cory, Erin Wolfson, and John Guy, you are legal champions that restored my faith in the justice system. Thank you for fighting the battle for our boys with sincerity of heart and total commitment. I will always be indebted to you for finding justice for Jordan, Leland, Tevin, and Tommie.

I am humbled by and grateful to my literary agent, Stuart Krichevsky, and my cowriter, Rosemarie Robotham, for your vision, support, humor, and love throughout this process. My book exists because of your faith in me to tell the story that had been written in my heart. You have truly been my "dream team." And to my editor, Dawn Davis, thank you for allowing me to speak my truth through this written account. I hope this book will be a source of strength to those who have lost loved ones to gun violence, and that it will offer inspiration that empowers them to live again.

Vicky Simmons, Lisa White, Angie Smith, and Anita Haymon, you are truly "my girls." Thank you for the many long hours of comforting woman-to-woman talks, and the movie nights and dinner dates that helped me to feel whole again. You continue to encourage, support, and love me as my life and work have taken on new meaning.

Derrick Moite, Vernell Johnson, Tawney Harden, and Dr. Twanna Estelle, I will never be able to repay you for your generosity, time, and effort on Jordan's behalf. In both his life and death you have shown us great love and kindness. And, to everyone who has ever prayed for Jordan and our family, or shed a tear on our behalf, I thank you from the deepest place in my heart. May God bless you all.

Notes

INTRODUCTION: IN GUNS WE TRUST

1. "Guns in Public Places," Everytown for Gun Safety, https://everytown research.org/issue/guns-in-public-places/ (accessed Oct. 13, 2017).

2. David Repass, "Gun Control Is Constitutional—Just Ask the Supreme Court," *The Hill*, October 18, 2017, http://thehill.com/opinion/civil-rights /356087-gun-control-is-constitutional-just-ask-the-supreme-court (accessed Feb. 24, 2018).

CHAPTER 2: CIVIL RIGHTS BABY

1. Tim Jones, "JFK Assassination Sowed Seeds of Failure For Gun-Control Efforts," *Chicago Tribune*, December 28, 2018, http://www.chicagotribune.com /news/sns-wp-blm-guns-4832d1f2-a97b-11e5-b596-113f59ee069a-20151226 -story.html (accessed Jul. 14, 2017).

2. Adam Winkler, "The Secret History of Guns," *The Atlantic*, September 2011, https://www.theatlantic.com/magazine/archive/2011/09/the-secret-history -of-guns/308608/ (accessed Jul. 22, 2017).

3. Dominic Erdozain, "Trump, Reagan and the NRA's Radical Agenda," CNN, April 27, 2017, http://www.cnn.com/2017/04/27/opinions/trump-aims-to -renew-special-bond-reagan-had-with-nra-opinion-erdozain/index.html (accessed Jul. 19, 2017).

4. Ibid.

5. Emily Wayrauch, "Black Kids Are 10 Times More Likely Than White Kids to Die from Guns," *Time*, June 20, 2017, http://time.com/4823524/gun-violence -black-children-study/ (accessed Nov. 8, 2017).

CHAPTER 3: STONES FROM THE RIVER

1. George H. W. Bush, *All the Best, George Bush: My Life in Letters and Other Writings* (New York: Scribner, 2000 reprint), p. 291.

CHAPTER 5: PAPER BOAT

1. Isabel Wilkerson, "No, You're Not Imagining It," *Essence*, September 2013, p. 132.
2. Ibid.
3. Ibid.
4. "Do Early Educators' Implicit Bias Regarding Sex and Race Relate to Behavior Expectations and Recommendations of Preschool Expulsions and Suspensions?" Yale University Child Study Center, September 28, 2016, p. 11, http://ziglercenter.yale.edu/publications/Preschool%20Implicit%20Bias%20 Policy%20Brief_final_9_26_276766_5379_v1.pdf.
5. Gaby Galvin, "Even Preschoolers Face Racial Bias, Study Finds," *US News*, September 28, 2016, https://www.usnews.com/news/articles/2016-09 -28/yale-study-finds-preschool-teachers-watch-black-boys-closer-for-bad -behavior (accessed Aug. 1, 2017).
6. Celeste Fremon and Stephanie Renfrow Hamilton, "Are Schools Failing Black Boys?," *Parenting*, April 1997, http://people.terry.uga.edu/dawndba/4500 FailingBlkBoys.html (accessed Jul. 26, 2017).

CHAPTER 8: FAST TRAPS

1. "Gun Violence by the Numbers," Everytown for Gun Safety, https://every townresearch.org/gun-violence-by-the-numbers/ (accessed Aug. 9, 2017).
2. Steve Kroft, "The Long-Shot Candidate," *60 Minutes*, February 2007, https:// www.youtube.com/watch?v=F8MxP9adPO8 (accessed Aug. 8, 2018).
3. Tom Murse, "List of Obama Gun Control Measures," ThoughtCo., February

21, 2018 (updated), https://www.thoughtco.com/obama-gun-laws-passed-by
-congress-3367595 (accessed Aug. 10, 2017).

4. Christopher Ingraham, "American Gun Ownership Drops to Lowest in Nearly
40 Years," *Washington Post*, June 29, 2016, https://www.washingtonpost.com
/news/wonk/wp/2016/06/29/american-gun-ownership-is-now-at-a-30-year
-low/?utm_term=.5c5ce2a9db0b (accessed May 28, 2017).

5. Christopher Ingraham, "Gun Sales Hit New Record Ahead of New Obama
Gun Restrictions," *Washington Post*, January 5, 2016, https://www.washington
post.com/news/wonk/wp/2016/01/05/gun-sales-hit-new-record-ahead-of
-new-obama-gun-restrictions/?tid=a_inl&utm_term=.ea032d2f7015 (accessed Nov. 4, 2017).

6. Lindsay Cook, "The NRA Should Send Obama a 'Thank You' Card," *US
News and World Report*, June 23, 2015, https://www.usnews.com/news/blogs
/data-mine/2015/06/23/the-nra-should-send-obama-a-thank-you-card (accessed Aug. 12, 2017).

7. Ibid.

8. "Gun Sales Soar During Obama's First Term: 'He Is the Best Thing That Ever Happened to the Firearm Industry,'" *The Blaze*, October 19, 2012, http://www.theblaze
.com/news/2012/10/19/gun-sales-soar-during-obamas-first-term-he-is-the-best
-thing-that-ever-happened-to-the-firearm-industry/ (accessed Aug. 15, 2017).

9. Cook, "The NRA Should Send Obama a 'Thank You' Card."

10. "3% of Americans Own Half the Country's 265 Million Guns," *USA Today*,
September 22, 2016, https://www.usatoday.com/story/news/2016/09/22
/study-guns-owners-violence/90858752/ (accessed Nov. 11, 2017).

11. "'The Color of Money' Expanded: Geographically Contingent Mortgage Lending in Atlanta," *Journal of Housing Research* vol. 12, no. 1 (2001), pp. 55–90,
http://www.jstor.org/stable/24833791?seq=1#page_scan_tab_contents (accessed Nov 10, 2017).

12. James Baldwin, *Notes of a Native Son* (Boston, MA: Beacon Press, 2012; reprint
of 1955 edition), pp. 113–14.

13. Phillip Goff, Matthew Jackson, Brooke Lewis Di Leone, Carmen Culotta, and
Natalie DiTomasso, "The Essence of Innocence: Consequences of Dehumanizing Black Children," *Journal of Personality and Social Psychology*, vol. 106,
no. 4 (2014), pp. 526–545, https://www.apa.org/pubs/journals/releases/psp
-a0035663.pdf.

14. Ibid.

15. Ibid.

16. Interview with Dr. Phillip Atiba Goff, conducted on March 6, 2014, by Rose-marie Robotham for "The State of the Black Family Survey," *Ebony*, June 2014.

17. Ibid.

CHAPTER 10: PREMONITION

1. Michael Harriot, "Open Letter to White People Who Are Obsessed with Black-on-Black Crime," *The Root*, August 4, 2016, https://www.theroot.com/open-letter-to-white-people-who-are-obsessed-with-black-1790856298 (accessed Nov. 3, 2017).

2. Michael Skolnik, "White People, You Will Never Look Suspicious Like Martin!" Global Grind, March 19, 2012, https://globalgrind.cassiuslife.com/1807268/michael-skolnik-trayvon-martin-george-zimmerman-race-sanford-florida-photos-pictures/ (accessed Oct. 23, 2017).

CHAPTER 11: TEN BULLETS

1. Marc Silver, dir., *3½ Minutes, Ten Bullets*, aired June 19, 2015, on HBO.

2. Paul Solotaroff, "A Most American Way to Die," *Rolling Stone*, April 25, 2013, http://www.rollingstone.com/culture/news/jordan-davis-stand-your-grounds-latest-victim-20130425 (accessed Aug. 13, 2017).

3. "The Meaning and Origin of the Expression: An Englishman's Home Is His Castle," Phrase Finder, http://www.phrases.org.uk/meanings/an-englishmans-home-is-his-castle.html (accessed Aug. 20, 2017).

4. Lily Rothman, "The Surprising History Behind America's Stand Your Ground Laws," *Time*, February 15, 2017, http://time.com/4664242/caroline-light-stand-your-ground-qa/ (accessed Oct. 25, 2017).

5. Ibid.

CHAPTER 13: A WIDER LENS

1. Barack Obama, Speech at the Prayer Vigil for Newtown Shooting Victims, December 16, 2012, Newtown, Connecticut, available at https://www

.washingtonpost.com/politics/president-obamas-speech-at-prayer-vigil
-for-newtown-shooting-victims-full-transcript/2012/12/16/f764bf8a-47dd
-11e2-ad54-580638ede391_story.html?utm_term=.5daca82803b6 (accessed
Sept. 23, 2017).

CHAPTER 14: EVERY MOM

1. Mark Follman, "Spitting, Stalking, Rape Threats: How Gun Extremists Target
   Women," *Mother Jones*, May 15, 2014, https://www.motherjones.com/politics
   /2014/05/guns-bullying-open-carry-women-moms-texas/ (accessed Feb. 25,
   2018).

2. Mark Follman, "These Women Are the NRA's Worst Nightmare," *Mother
   Jones*, September/October 2014, http://www.motherjones.com/politics
   /2014/09/moms-demand-action-guns-madd-shannon-watts-nra/ (accessed
   Oct. 28, 2017).

3. Ibid.

4. Ibid.

5. "Innocents Lost: A Year of Unintentional Child Gun Deaths," Everytown for
   Gun Safety and Moms Demand Action for Gun Sense in America, June 2014,
   https://everytownresearch.org/documents/2015/04/innocents-lost.pdf (accessed Nov. 30, 2017).

6. Ibid.

7. "Mass Shootings in the United States: 2009-2016," Everytown for Gun Safety,
   April 11, 2017, https://everytownresearch.org/reports/mass-shootings-analysis/
   (accessed Nov. 30, 2017).

8. Ibid.

9. Follman, "These Women Are the NRA's Worst Nightmare."

CHAPTER 16: THE COLOR OF JUSTICE

1. Jelani Cobb, "George Zimmerman, Not Guilty: Blood on the Leaves," *New
   Yorker*, July 13, 2013, https://www.newyorker.com/news/news-desk/george
   -zimmerman-not-guilty-blood-on-the-leaves (accessed Sept. 25, 2017).

2. Michael Dunn to Rhonda Rouer, letter, June 22, 2013, http://floridajustice.com
   /michael-dunns-letters-from-jail/ (accessed Sept. 25, 2017).

CHAPTER 17: A JURY OF HIS PEERS

1. Mark Berman, "Juror from the Michael Dunn trial explains the deadlock," *Washington Post*, February 20, 2014, https://www.washingtonpost.com/news/post-nation/wp/2014/02/20/juror-from-the-michael-dunn-trial-explains-the-deadlock/?utm_term=.040fab0ada36 (accessed Oct. 9, 2017).

2. Seni Tienabeso, "Juror in 'Loud Music' Trial Wanted Murder Conviction," ABC News, February 19, 2014, http://abcnews.go.com/US/juror-loud-music-trial-wanted-murder-conviction/story?id=22571068 (accessed Oct. 9, 2017).

3. Michael Dunn to his grandmother, letter, February 20, 2013, http://floridajustice.com/wp-content/uploads/2013/02/LetterJ.pdf (accessed Oct. 10, 2017).

4. Michael Dunn to Rhonda Rouer, letter, June 22, 2013, http://floridajustice.com/michael-dunns-letters-from-jail/ (accessed Sept. 25, 2017).

5. Michael Dunn to his daughter, letter, July 12, 2013, https://floridajustice.com/wp-content/uploads/2013/02/LetterK.pdf (accessed Sept. 25, 2017).

6. John Phillips, "Michael Dunn: What His Former Neighbor Had to Say About Him," Law Offices of John Phillips, http://floridajustice.com/michaeldunn (accessed Oct. 10, 2017).

7. Marc Silver, dir., *3½ Minutes, Ten Bullets*, aired June 19, 2015, on HBO.

CHAPTER 18: GOD, THE PROTECTOR

1. Rachel Kaadzi Ghansah, "A Most American Terrorist: The Making of Dylann Roof." *GQ*, August 21, 2017, https://www.gq.com/story/dylann-roof-making-of-an-american-terrorist (accessed Apr. 17, 2018).

2. Rob Schenck, "An Evangelical Minister on Why American Evangelicals Are Wrong About Gun Control," *Vice*, January 25, 2016, https://news.vice.com/article/an-evangelical-minister-rob-schenck-on-why-american-evangelicals-are-wrong-about-gun-control (accessed Oct. 14, 2017).

3. Ibid.

4. Chris Williams, "The Strange Love Affair Between Christians and Guns," Patheos, June 14, 2016, http://www.patheos.com/blogs/chrisicisms/2016/06/14/christians-and-guns/ (accessed October 14, 2017).

5. Evan Defilippis and Devin Hughes, "New Study Is Latest to Find That Higher Rates of Gun Ownership Lead to Higher Rates of Violent Crime," The Trace, https://www.thetrace.org/2015/06/new-study-is-latest-to-find-that-higher-rates-of-gun-ownership-lead-to-higher-rates-of-violent-crime/ (accessed May 27, 2017).

6. Ibid.

7. "Gun Violence by the Numbers," Everytown for Gun Safety, https://everytownresearch.org/gun-violence-by-the-numbers (accessed Dec. 29, 2017).

8. Ibid.

9. Ibid.

CHAPTER 19: HOPE DEALERS

1. Alexandra Filinara and Noah Kaplan, "Racial Resentment and Whites' Gun Policy Preferences in Contemporary America," Academia, p. 1, http://www.academia.edu/16785113/Racial_Resentment_and_White_Americans_Gun_Policy_Preferences (accessed Oct. 16, 2017).

2. Melissa Batchelor Warnke, "Sandra Bland, Philando Castile and Now Charleena Lyles. Scream Their Names for All to Hear," *Los Angeles Times*, June 19, 2017, http://www.latimes.com/opinion/opinion-la/la-ol-castille-charleena-lyles-police-shooting-20170619-story.html (accessed Nov. 6, 2017).

3. Michael A. Cohen, "Why Won't the NRA Speak Out About Philando Castile?" *Boston Globe*, June 20, 2017, https://www.bostonglobe.com/opinion/2017/06/20/why-won-nra-speak-out-about-philando-castile/6P6pIx7bHRQ0Zlw FJ7x4VJ/story.html (accessed Oct. 14, 2017).

4. "Everytown, Moms Demand Action Release Report Highlighting Overlooked 2017 Trend in State Capitals Across the Country: Gun Safety Victories," Moms Demand Gun Sense in America, June 13, 2017, https://momsdemandaction.org/in-the-news/everytown-moms-demand-action-release-report-highlighting-overlooked-2017-trend-in-state-capitals-across-the-country-gun-safety-victories/ (accessed Oct. 18, 2017).

5. Ibid.

6. Ibid.

7. Ibid.

8. Ibid.

9. Michael McBride, "Gun Violence, Race and the Church," Faith & Leadership, February 7, 2017, https://www.faithandleadership.com/michael-mcbride-gun -violence-race-and-church (accessed Nov. 11, 2017).

CHAPTER 20: SAY THEIR NAMES

1. Mike Spies and Ashley Balcerzak, "The NRA Placed Big Bets on the 2016 Election, and Won Almost All of Them," OpenSecrets Blog and the Trace, November 9, 2016, https://www.huffingtonpost.com/opensecrets-blog/the -nra-placed-big-bets-o_b_12888600.html (accessed Oct. 19, 2017).